Colonial Settlements in America

Jamestown
New Amsterdam
Philadelphia
Plymouth
St. Augustine
Santa Fe
Williamsburg
Yerba Buena

Williamsburg

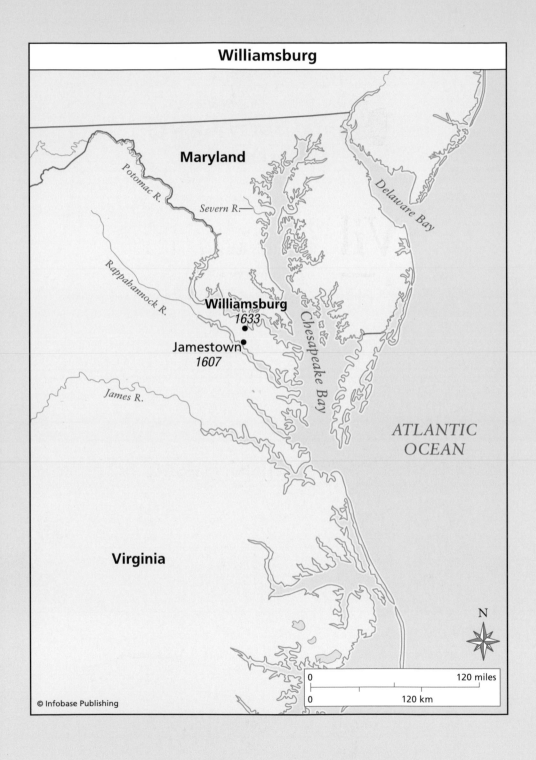

Maryland

Potomac R.

Severn R.

Rappahannock R.

Williamsburg
1633

Jamestown
1607

James R.

Chesapeake Bay

Delaware Bay

Virginia

ATLANTIC
OCEAN

N

0		120 miles
0		120 km

© Infobase Publishing

COLONIAL SETTLEMENTS
IN AMERICA

Williamsburg

Tim McNeese

CHELSEA HOUSE
PUBLISHERS

An imprint of Infobase Publishing

Frontis: Originally known as Middle Plantation, Williamsburg was settled in 1633, and from 1699 to 1780, it served as Virginia's capital.

Williamsburg

Copyright © 2007 by Infobase Publishing

Chelsea House
An imprint of Infobase Publishing
132 West 31st Street
New York, NY 10001

ISBN-10: 0-7910-9333-6
ISBN-13: 978-0-7910-9333-7

Library of Congress Cataloging-in-Publication Data
McNeese, Tim.
 Williamsburg / Tim McNeese.
   p. cm. — (Colonial settlements in America)
 Includes bibliographical references and index.
 Audience: Grades 7–8.
 ISBN 0-7910-9333-6 (hardcover)
   1. Williamsburg (Va.)—History—Juvenile literature. 2. Virginia—History—Colonial period, ca. 1600-1775—Juvenile literature. I. Title. II. Series.
 F234.W7M38 2007
 975.5'4252—dc22   2006028366

Series design by Erika K. Arroyo
Cover design by Ben Peterson

Printed in the United States of America

Bang EJB 10 9 8 7 6 5 4 3 2 1

This book is printed on acid-free paper.

Contents

1

Conflict in Virginia

On a Sunday morning in July 1675, a group of Virginia col-onists, on their way to church, came upon a gruesome sight. Passing a local plantation, the passers by spotted two men lying on the ground. One, a Native American, was already dead. The other, a local herdsman named Robert Hen, was close to death. The two men had been "chopped on their heads, arms and other part, as if done with Indian hatchets."[1]

As the church-bound colonists rushed toward the bleeding Hen, he spoke the same word twice: "Doegs! Doegs!"[2] Just as Hen breathed his last, a young boy came out of the colonist's cabin and excitedly explained that, "Indians had come at the break of day and done these murders."[3] Word of the murders spread quickly up and down the Potomac River Valley and beyond. Angry colonists wasted little time avenging the death of one of their own.

Robert Hen's dying reference to "Doegs" was to a local Indian tribe that lived north of the Potomac River, in the neighboring colony of Maryland. There had been problems lately between some colonists and the Doegs. After a Virginian named Thomas Mathew had failed to pay a party of Doegs for some trade items, they raided his plantation and stole some hogs as payment. Colonists responded by tracking the raiders down and killing a couple of them. Now, the Doegs seemingly returned the favor by attacking the Potomac plantation where Hen lived. Mathew owned the plantation that was attacked that bloody July day.

MISPLACED VENGEANCE

Virginia militiamen were called out to respond to the latest killings. As they marched in pursuit of the Doegs, they split up into two groups. One group soon caught up with the guilty warriors upriver on the Maryland side of the Potomac. A militia raid resulted in the deaths of 10 Doegs, including their leader. The militiamen were pleased with their success, and they did not care that what they had done was illegal. Their attack had taken place on Maryland soil, which they had invaded illegally. Also, they could not have been certain that the warriors they had just killed were, in fact, the party that had murdered Hen.

But the militiamen had not yet made their worst mistake. The second group of Virginia soldiers soon attacked a group of Native Americans at another nearby site. There, 14 Native Americans were shot down by militiamen before one of the Native Americans shouted out two shocking words: "Susquehanougs Netoughs! Susquehannah friends!"[4] The avenging colonists had attacked the wrong group of Native Americans; they had attacked the peaceful Susquehanna tribe. It was a mistake the colonial troops would soon regret.

The militia attack on the Susquehannas soon escalated to new violence on the Virginia frontier. Just as the Virginians had sought revenge for the death of Robert Hen, the Susquehannas now wanted a bloody revenge of their own. Meanwhile, back in Jamestown, the colonial capital of Virginia, a second drama

Sir William Berkeley was appointed governor of Virginia in 1641
by King Charles I of England. During the first three decades of his
governorship, he fostered a peaceful relationship with local Native
Americans, largely because he had a vested interest in the fur trade.

would soon unfold. Following the Virginia militia raid north of
the Potomac, the Maryland governor protested to the governor
of Virginia, Sir William Berkeley. Berkeley responded by ordering an investigation.

For more than three decades, Berkeley had worked hard to maintain peaceful relations with the Native Americans of the region. He had been governor of Virginia several times since the 1640s. He was certainly not new to dealing with conflicts between Native Americans and the settlers in his colony. He had gained a reputation as a forceful leader during earlier conflicts. Those years had passed, however. Berkeley was tired of Virginia and of leading the commonwealth. He longed to return to England.

Berkeley's investigation never took place. Instead, the militia officers Berkeley ordered to hold an inquiry called for a second raid against the Susquehannas. They even requested help from the Maryland militia. Soon, 1,000 militia troops from both colonies massed together and attacked the Susquehannas' main encampment, a fort they had constructed along the Potomac. The attack took place in September. (Before the attack, the militiamen pretended they wanted to council with the Susquehanna leaders. When four chiefs came out to talk, they were hacked to death with axes.) In the weeks that followed, fighting between the Susquehannas in the fort and the colonial militia troops raged. Several colonial soldiers were killed. When the troops finally asked to sit down and talk with the Susquehanna, their enemies responded: "Where are our four *Cockarouses* (Great Men)?"[5] Finally, the Susquehannas left their fort under cover of darkness, eluding the Virginia and Maryland militiamen. When the smoke of the battles cleared, the colonials had lost 50 men.

A GOVERNOR'S MISSTEPS

Back in Jamestown, Governor Berkeley was furious. His orders had not been obeyed and, even worse, the Susquehannas were now roaming the frontier in small, scattered bands, looking for blood. In the months that followed, Susquehannas raided isolated colonial settlements, killing or capturing nearly 40 people, burning some and skinning others alive. Governor Berkeley ordered a unit of militiamen to go and battle the Susquehannas. But, before they were sent out, he changed his mind and disbanded them. Strangely, the governor gave no reason. Then, in January 1676, the Susquehanna leader sued for peace. He explained that his people had killed 10 colonists for each of their four Cockarouses. But it was too late. The colonists were not going to accept a peaceful settlement.

In March, Governor Berkeley called a special session of the House of Burgesses. He pushed through an act that called for a declaration of war against the Susquehannas. A string of protective forts would be built along the frontier to protect those living in the backwoods. A militia force of 500 men was raised. Militia horse patrols would watch the territory between the forts for any signs of Native Americans. Finally, Berkeley wanted to avoid another situation similar to the one that had opened the violence the previous winter. To that end, he ordered that no attack against a Native American village or fort should take place without his direct permission. Troops were not even to fire on Native Americans without approval from Berkeley. To Berkeley, who wanted to control the violence on the frontier, his policy made perfect sense. To those living in fear on the frontier, Berkeley's policy "made about as much sense . . . as trench warfare would against helicopters and paratroops."[6]

Virginia frontiersmen and their families were angered by Berkeley's overly cautious policy. They knew that Berkeley was not just interested in pursuing peace and order on the frontier. They knew he wanted to protect the lucrative pelt trade. For years, the governor and his agents had engaged in a highly profitable trade in beaver and otter skins with the Susquehannas. The frontier residents felt their safety was taking a back seat to the fur trade. "No bullits [must] pierse beaver skins!" became the backswoods cry of protest.[7] The colonials felt they could no longer rely on their governor for protection. They would take matters into their own hands. When, in March 1676, word spread along the frontier that Native Americans were gathering for a massive attack, many fearful backcountry settlers gathered along the James River at a place called Jordan's Point (near present-day Hopewell). This collection of angry frontiersmen needed someone to lead them. They soon chose Nathaniel Bacon, Jr., the former master of a frontier plantation whose overseer had been killed by Native Americans. He and Lord Berkeley would soon find themselves locked in a test of wills, one that would lead to the decline in importance for Jamestown and the rise in the significance of a new capital site. That site was known as Middle Plantation. Another generation would know it as Williamsburg.

2

Bacon Leads the Fight

Nathaniel Bacon, Jr., had arrived in Virginia just three years earlier. He was a short, slim man in his late 20s, with coal-black hair. He had come to America following some financial setbacks in England. But Bacon was no commoner. In fact, he and Berkeley were similar in several ways. They both were descended from wealthy, upper-class English families. They both were university-educated, Berkeley at Oxford and Bacon at Cambridge. Both men were scholars, extremely proud, and had quick tempers. In fact, Berkeley and Bacon were related as cousins by marriage. But while Bacon was not yet 30 years old, Berkeley was almost 70.

Once he arrived in America, Nathaniel Bacon, Jr., soon found his niche. Another cousin, Nathaniel Bacon, Sr., was a member of Governor Berkeley's Virginia Council. Not long after arriving in Virginia, Bacon was appointed to the council. He became a New World planter, settling on a plantation located about 40 miles upriver from Jamestown. Soon, he acquired a second plantation that he called "Bacon's Quarter."

Due to Governor William Berkeley's policy of not allowing Virginia residents to attack Native Americans without first obtaining his permission, those living on the frontier looked for a leader who wasn't afraid to retaliate when attacked. The frontiersmen selected Nathaniel Bacon, Jr., (depicted here) as their leader, but his actions were quickly denounced by Governor Berkeley.

That tobacco farm stood on the edge of the Virginia frontier, and it was there that Bacon's overseer was killed by the Susquehannas. Recognized as one of the important planters in the region, Bacon was well regarded by the local frontiersmen and farmers who turned to him for leadership. Bacon enthusiastically accepted their support.

AN UNOFFICIAL LEADER

Although Bacon made decisions on behalf of those willing to follow him, he did so with no official authority. He did make application for a formal commission from Governor Berkeley, but was turned down. Instead, Berkeley declared Bacon a threat to the peace, calling him and his followers "rebells and mutineers."[8] The governor even set out up the James River with some soldiers, intent on arresting Bacon and his men. By the time he arrived at the Bacon plantation, the "rebells" were long gone. They were headed along the Traders' Path, to the south, in search of the Susquehannas.

Along the way, Bacon tried to enlist the help of other Indian tribes against the Susquehannas. But he had no such luck until he reached the camps of the Occaneechee, an Indian group located along the Virginia–North Carolina border. This group of Native Americans had traditionally been friendly with the Virginia colonists and were the middlemen in the beaver trade between Jamestown and tribes located farther south. The Occaneechees told Bacon and his men that the Susquehannas were hiding just a few miles away. The Occaneechees then agreed to attack the Susquehannas, an offer that Bacon accepted. But once Bacon's Native American allies defeated his enemy, he and his men turned on them. Why Bacon's forces attacked the cooperating Occaneechees is not clear. They may have needed food for their return trip, which the Occaneechees had refused to give them. Bacon may have had his eye on a giant stack of beaver pelts the Occaneechees had accumulated from a winters worth of trapping. His men may have just wanted to attack some Native Americans on their own. Whatever the reason, the Virginians attacked the

Occaneechees, an attack that turned into a massacre of men, women, and children.

Bacon and his men soon returned to their homes in the James River region. Although they had "succeeded" in defeating the Susquehannas (even if the Occaneechees had done the fighting for them), Governor Berkeley was not pleased. He drafted a strong statement against Bacon, which he issued on May 10, 1676, and removed Bacon from his council seat. But Berkeley soon understood that Bacon had become a hero to many of those who lived under the threat of attack. Berkeley dissolved the sitting House of Burgesses, calling for new elections, something he had not done in 15 years! To satisfy the will of the common people, he allowed all freemen to vote, a privilege previously restricted to property owners. Berkeley also offered to pardon Bacon for his rebellious actions, if the plantation gentleman agreed to apologize. Bacon, of course, refused.

A DISAPPOINTED BERKELEY

When the election for the new House of Burgesses was held, Governor Berkeley was disappointed with the outcome. The commoners had voted for many of Bacon's followers, as well as for Bacon himself. The next month, the new members of the House of Burgesses were to gather in Jamestown. Bacon left his plantation and took a small sloop down the James River to the colonial capital, accompanied by 30 armed followers. He had his boat docked out of cannon range of Jamestown, uncertain how he would be received by Governor Berkeley. His doubts about a warm welcome from the governor were soon confirmed. Berkeley sent a larger ship, the *Adam and Eve*, to capture Bacon and bring him onboard his smaller ship. Soon, Bacon was a prisoner standing before Governor Berkeley. Upon seeing Bacon, the governor threw his hands into the air and cried: "Now I behold the greatest rebel that ever was in Virginia!"[9] Despite Berkeley's anger with Bacon, he soon offered the gentleman rebel amnesty if he would admit his disobedience against the governor's earlier orders. Two days after his arrest, Bacon agreed, writing out his confession and handing it to Lord Berkeley. With this behind them, Lord Berkeley restored Bacon to his seat on the governor's council and even promised to grant Bacon a "Commission to Gett volunteers to Goe against the Indians."[10] In a way, Berkeley may not have had a choice. When he took Bacon prisoner, the streets of Jamestown were soon filled with 2,000 of Bacon's followers who were upset and angered by their leader's capture by the governor.

Berkeley's moves might have brought an end to the conflict between himself and Bacon. But it was not to be. When Bacon's commission papers were not presented, he and his followers began to doubt Berkeley's sincerity. By the following month, Bacon, who was back at his plantation at Henrico, prepared to take matters again into his own hands. Only this time, his target was not the Native Americans, but Berkeley himself. On June 23, Bacon and 400 of his followers marched on Jamestown. Bacon was intent on demanding his commission from Berkeley. His men were ready for action. Bacon would get his official commission to lead them or they would "pull down the Towne."[11]

A high and intense drama played itself out on the streets of the Virginia capital. When Berkeley came out of the statehouse to meet Bacon, anxious burgesses watched from the windows of the colonial building. Jamestown had not grown much in population over the previous 50 years. But many of the old, original buildings were no longer there. Instead, they had been replaced by more permanent, brick structures. The statehouse had been built in the early 1660s. It was composed of a row of brick buildings that faced the James River. These government buildings included rooms for the colony's House

Although Governor William Berkeley deemed Nathaniel Bacon a traitor when Bacon attacked the Occaneechees without his permission, Berkeley offered him amnesty and a commission in return for admitting his guilt. Bacon agreed, but when he didn't receive his commission, he led 400 of his followers to Jamestown to confront Berkeley (which is depicted in this engraving).

of Burgesses, the governor's council, and the governor's own official chambers.

The Virginia governor angrily taunted the would-be rebel. He bared his chest and begged Bacon: "Here! Shoot me! Before God, a fair mark! Shoot!"[12] Bacon, of course, refused and stated his reason for coming back to Jamestown was not to "hurt a hair on your head,"[13] but only to get the commission the governor had promised. Berkeley refused. Then the governor turned his back on Bacon and began to walk back into the statehouse. His temper raging, Bacon ordered his men to cock their pistols and point them toward the government house. "I'll kill governor, council, assembly and all," shouted Bacon, "and then I'll sheath my sword in my own heart's blood."[14]

DRAMATIC CONFRONTATIONS

With almost no one in Jamestown willing to back the governor, Bacon and his men soon had free rein of the town. The frightened burgesses surrendered to Bacon and his mob. They gave him his commission, making him "General of the Virginia War." As for Berkeley, he had no choice but to agree. But Bacon was not satisfied with just a commission for himself. He came back the following day, requesting blank commissions for officers to serve under his command, saying he would fill them in later. He wanted some of Berkeley's followers dismissed from their offices and also letters to be sent to the king justifying every step he had taken against the Native Americans and the leaders in Jamestown. Again, Berkeley, his back against the wall, had no choice. Bacon received everything he asked for. Soon, he was planning a new war against the Native Americans. He was the new power in Virginia. As one eyewitness lamented: "Now, tagg, ragg, & bobtayle carry a high hand."[15]

To his followers, Bacon's commission could not have come at a better time. Within days, the mob in Jamestown received word of an attack by Native Americans 23 miles upriver. Another eight colonists had been killed. Bacon gathered his men, "flags were unfurled, drums sounded, and he marched away at the head of his troops."[16] As Bacon's makeshift army advanced, his "officers" used their power to confiscate supplies from local wealthy planters along the way. When the planters complained to Berkeley, he believed that Bacon was losing his power and his following. He could not have been more wrong. Berkeley rode out of Jamestown, intent on rallying rural colonists against Bacon. But few sided with the already discredited governor. When news of Berkeley's recruitment plans reached Bacon, he gathered his men and began moving in search of the governor. Receiving word that he, not the Native Americans, had become the hunted, Governor Berkeley fled the colony, crossing Chesapeake Bay, and taking refuge on the Eastern Shore of Virginia. With the governor having abandoned the colony of Virginia, the entire region around Jamestown was in the hands of Nathaniel Bacon and his men.

Bacon used the opportunity to establish his power. At what was known as Middle Plantation, Bacon held a political meeting. He wrote out an oath of loyalty for his supporters to swear by. On August 3, Bacon issued an "official" document, the "Manifesto and Declaration of the People." In it, he accused Berkeley of lining his pockets through the beaver trade and arming Native Americans who had already murdered colonists. Berkeley had to be arrested and stand trial. In the meantime, Bacon promised to pursue all Native Americans that threatened the colony. For the first time, Bacon appeared intent on leading a political revolution against the established power of the Virginia colony. Few wealthy planters took Bacon's oath. But many others—backwoodsmen, commoners, poor farmers—did so. They had little to lose and, perhaps, a new status to gain in the colony that Bacon seemed to be controlling. To further his power, Bacon called for elections of a new House of Burgesses that would meet in Jamestown on September 4. Following these moves, Bacon and several hundred of his men went out in search of Native Americans. They did not find those they were looking for. Instead, they stumbled onto the Pamunkeys, who were peaceful. Fighting in a swamp, the colonists killed eight Pamunkeys and captured 45. Although he had attacked the wrong tribe, Bacon chalked his campaign up to another victory against troublesome Native Americans.

It was then that Bacon received word that Berkeley had returned and taken control of Jamestown once again. (Bacon had

A LITTLE TOO MUCH WINE

The conflict between Lord Berkeley, governor of the Virginia colony, and Nathaniel Bacon, a wealthy planter, eventually became a monumental struggle between two forceful men. Although Bacon gained widespread support in his attempt to take control of Jamestown and the entire colony, Berkeley finally won. There are important reasons why. One of them had to do with a ship's captain who may have consumed too much wine.

Prior to Bacon's Rebellion, Lord Berkeley had served off and on as Virginia's governor for 26 years. Berkeley himself was as old as Jamestown, having been born in 1607. He had first been appointed as royal governor the year Nathaniel Bacon was born! Although he was much older than Bacon, he was not without resources in facing down the Virginia planter and his followers.

But defeating Bacon was not an easy process. More than once, due to the number of Bacon's supporters, Berkeley was forced to leave Jamestown and take refuge on the Eastern Shore, which was across Chesapeake Bay. This proved to be a shrewd move by the governor. But it also made him vulnerable. It was during Berkeley's second escape from Jamestown that Bacon sent forces to capture the governor. Bacon was able to commandeer the only two or three large merchant vessels docked at Jamestown for his own use. He had cannon placed on them from the Jamestown fort. He then sent his small fleet to the Eastern Shore with orders to seize Berkeley.

Berkeley managed to turn the tables on Bacon's plan, however. When Bacon's ships sailed the 30 miles across the Chesapeake, Berkeley sent a request to the captain of the fleet to sit down and negotiate his surrender. While meeting with the governor, the ship's captain was given wine to drink. As Berkeley continued ordering more wine for the captain, a small boatload of his supporters rowed out to the largest of Bacon's confiscated ships. Soon, Berkeley's men seized the ship. The English sailors onboard were not from Virginia, and they were all too willing to help Berkeley against the rebel who had captured their vessel in the first place. With Bacon's ships now his own, Berkeley and his men were able to retake Jamestown.

Without ships, Bacon's efforts would ultimately fail. Virginia in 1676 was as much a water-based colony as a land-based one. Whoever controlled the waterways would control the outcome of the conflict. And, by offering one ship's captain too much wine, Berkeley gained the advantage.

sent some men on a captured ship to take Berkeley prisoner only to have the ship's captain turn on Bacon's men and then deliver the governor back to Jamestown.) Bacon wasted little time turning around and marching a second time on the colonial capital. By September 13, the rebel leader and his followers were outside the town at a site called Green Spring, an old Native American field. Here, Bacon rallied his men: "Come on, my hearts of gold," he shouted in a stirring voice. "He that dies in the field lies in the bed of honor!"[17]

A MARCH ON JAMESTOWN

Bacon and his "army" approached Jamestown through a waterway known as the Great Dragon Swamp. Berkeley's handful of loyal followers had already fortified the corridor with three cannon and a wooden fort. Bacon responded by ordering his men to dig fortifications for protection. But the work was slow, because his men only had two axes and one spade among them. To keep Berkeley from firing on his exposed location, Bacon ordered some of his men to go out and round up the wives of some of the wealthy planters who were supporting Berkeley. The women were forced to stand between Berkeley's forces and Bacon's men. This gave Bacon and his fellow rebels time to complete their fortifications. Then the women were released.

On September 15, the long-standing conflict between Bacon and Berkeley erupted into a small-scale battle. Guns blazed from Berkeley's fort and from ships lined up along the James River. But there was little enthusiasm among Berkeley's followers. When three cannon arrived to support Bacon's defensive line, Berkeley's men spiked their guns and abandoned their position. Jamestown was once more at the mercy of Nathaniel Bacon.

From a ship on the river, Governor Berkeley watched helplessly as Bacon's men entered the town and put it to the torch

On September 19, 1676, Nathaniel Bacon burned down Virginia's capital, Jamestown—the last major act of his rebellion. Shortly after this event, Bacon's support began to wane and a temporary capital was established at Williamsburg, 12 miles to the northeast.

on September 19. Every building in Jamestown, old and new, was destroyed by fire, including the settlement's church. Bacon waited to set the fires until after sundown and Berkeley, from his place on a ship's deck, "could see the fires light the harvest sky."[18] Bacon and his men had managed to symbolically unseat Virginia's colonial government and actually burn the capitol building itself. Jamestown would never recover from this wholesale destruction. Although no one knew what Bacon's actions would mean for Virginia's future, his rebellion set a course that would lead to the establishment of another colonial settlement, one that would in a few short years become the new capital of the Tidewater colony—Williamsburg.

3

Recovery from Rebellion

The events that surrounded Nathaniel Bacon's small-scale revolution against Virginia's colonial authorities took place after nearly 70 years of English colonizing in the Western Hemisphere. Seven decades earlier, English colonists and settlers, investors and adventurers had sailed to the New World to add their contributions to the expansion of the British Empire. Although some European powers had first colonized parts of the Americas in the late 1400s, the English established their first successful colony in the Western Hemisphere in 1607, with the landing of three small ships carrying fewer than 150 men and boys.

They had landed in the region of the Tidewater, with plans to build a base of operation on behalf of their sovereign, King James I. The ships had reached the mouth of the James River that spring, and a settlement site was soon selected. Through the decades that followed, their New World outpost—first called Fort James and later called Jamestown—"served as the seat of government and administrative center of England's largest colony in North America."[19]

AFTER THE REBELLION

The burning of Jamestown by an ego-driven Nathaniel Bacon would mark the end of his revolt against Governor Berkeley. His support began to wane. Some of Bacon's followers, now out of control, began to loot local plantations. The drive for revolution in Virginia petered out, reduced to little more than mobs who "ran off cattle, took fence rails for firewood . . . invaded houses and wantonly destroyed furnishings."[20] Berkeley again took refuge on the Eastern Shore, across Chesapeake Bay. Because he controlled all the local ships, Bacon's men could not reach him. Berkeley was still the governor, and Bacon was being reduced to little more than the former leader of an increasingly destructive and unruly mob of frontiersmen. Perhaps fortunately, in October, Bacon became extremely ill with the "bloody flux," or dysentery. (He was also infested with lice.) He died on October 26. His grave was hidden and has never been uncovered. With Bacon's death, the rebellion was over. Berkeley soon regained control of his colony, and the rebels who had so enthusiastically followed the magnetic Nathaniel Bacon were suddenly without their leader.

But all did not end well for Governor Berkeley. Once his power was restored, he set out on a course of revenge against anyone he believed had been a part of Bacon's Rebellion. He ordered captured rebels to be tried and executed. (It was a common practice to have the guilty drawn and quartered, their bodies pulled apart by horses.) Rebel lands and estates were confiscated by Berkeley's agents and their families put out to starve. Lord Berkeley's revenge proved so severe that King Charles II turned on his royal governor. Charles noted: "That old fool has hanged more men in that naked country than I have done for the murder of my father!" (Charles II's father, King Charles I, had been executed following an English revolution in the 1640s.) Although Berkeley had beaten Bacon and put down his rebellion, by January 1677, an English fleet arrived on the James

In retaliation for those who opposed him during Bacon's Rebellion, Governor William Berkeley ordered that all rebels be tried and executed. This wood engraving depicts the wife of Edmund Cheeseman, who is depicted here fainting after Berkeley ordered her husband to the gallows for his role in the rebellion.

River, docking near the burned-out remains of Jamestown, to report to Berkeley that he was no longer governor of Virginia. Berkeley took passage on a ship to England to explain himself to the king, but died a month after his arrival in London, having never gained an audience with Charles II.

THE ORIGINS OF WILLIAMSBURG

The history of Williamsburg, which would one day become the capital of colonial Virginia, "really began at seventeenth-century Jamestown."[21] From its founding in 1607 through the next 90 years, Jamestown served the English colony of Virginia. Situated along the banks of the James River, early Jamestown was a busy site founded on struggle and hard-won survival. Hundreds of excited and hopeful English colonists, including not only men, but women and children, came to the shores of Chesapeake Bay and made their way up the James River to find a new place for themselves in the New World. Over and over, hundreds of these colonists died, victims of silent killers, such as mosquito-borne malaria, and of the Native Americans who attacked, sometimes with great ferocity.

But the English, despite such losses, clung to their toehold in America and managed to establish a colony rooted in sweat, blood, and the profits from tobacco. Throughout the 1600s, colonists fanned out from Jamestown, establishing farms and tobacco plantations up and down a half dozen Virginia rivers from the James to the York, the Chickahominy to the Rappahannock. With each passing decade of the seventeenth century, the larger commonwealth of Virginia grew. However, the settlement site of Jamestown did not. Even though it was never abandoned completely throughout the 1600s, Jamestown remained a difficult place to live. Early on, the site gained "a notorious reputation as a disease-ridden, indefensible settlement."[22]

JAMESTOWN'S SHAKY FUTURE

With the burning of Jamestown by the revolutionary Nathaniel Bacon and his supporters, the future of England's first successful colonial settlement in America was in doubt. Jamestown had always been a colonial community with significant problems. Many had to do with the settlement's location. It was established along the James River at a location that English ships could easily reach. The colonists who had founded the site in 1607 had also chosen the location because it was an island, one easily defended against attacks by Native Americans. But other problems plagued the site. It was on low ground, amid swampy water. The island's water supply was poor, with its groundwater

Strategically located on an island, Jamestown was a safe haven for Virginia's first settlers. However, the settlement's location was also a detriment—the low, swampy ground ensured that the water supply was poor and that millions of mosquitoes tormented colonists by spreading malaria.

eventually polluted with human waste. The swamp was a breeding ground for millions of mosquitoes that tormented the colonists in summer and spread deadly malaria among the residents of Jamestown. Although it had served as the original colony for the English in Virginia, Jamestown had never been a popular place to live. By the end of the seventeenth century, Jamestown's days were numbered as the colonial capital of English Virginia.

The settlement site that would, in time, replace Jamestown, not only as the most important colonial settlement in Virginia, but as the capital, would be known as Williamsburg. Before the site was named after the English monarch King William, it was known as Middle Plantation. This early Virginia site, which branched off from Jamestown, was situated in the wilderness region between the James and York rivers, as close to one as the other. Its first settlers arrived in 1633. The site was authorized for settlement by the then-Virginia governor John Harvey. The petition for colonizing was approved by the House of Burgesses, the colonial legislature in Virginia, as well as the governor's council in Jamestown. The document was referred to as "An Act for the Seatinge of the Middle Plantation."[23] The legislation that authorized the establishment of a town at Middle Plantation noted the difference in terrain and environment compared to Jamestown, citing Middle Plantation's "serene and temperate air." The act also mentioned that those who had already settled there found the site to be "healthy, and agreeable to their constitutions."[24]

The newly authorized Middle Plantation was to be located along two tributaries of the York and James rivers. Queen's Creek, flowing into the York, would flank the new settlement on the north, while Archer's Hope Creek would run south of the site into the James River. These two creeks would be important to any settlers moving to the region. Despite Jamestown's drawbacks, its location on the James River gave oceangoing ships easy access to its docks for trade and tobacco shipments. But Queen's and Archer's Hope creeks could also be accessed by smaller vessels, called sloops, that could easily reach any planter's local wharf, take on large barrels (known as hogsheads) filled with tobacco, and sail down either the York or the James and transfer their cargoes onto larger ships for transport to distant markets.

A WALL FOR DEFENSE

The act authorizing Middle Plantation called for the settlers to construct a fort wall, or palisade, of wooden logs. This was intended as a barrier to keep local Native Americans from advancing onto the lower peninsula. It also would add to the already existing fort walls that had been built along the James River. To make certain the proposed palisade was constructed, the Virginia burgesses ordered that 1 in every 40 male colonists was to prepare to move to Middle Plantation, at least temporarily, to take up the planned efforts of "securing that Tract of Land lyinge betweene the sayd Creekes."[25]

But even though the protective fort barrier was built, it was not adequately maintained over the years. By 1644, it had fallen down in several places and was in a serious state of disrepair and rot. That year, the local Native Americans organized a massive uprising. Several Virginia colonists were killed and many others terrorized by this new wave of violence. Again, Virginia officials leaped into action. New work was started on rebuilding the worn-out, ineffective palisade. A local planter named Richard Higgenson was hired to oversee the reworking of the old fort wall at Middle Plantation. Some portions were simply restored, while others required the building of a whole new palisade.

Once again, the English colonists had built their line of separation between themselves and the Native Americans in the region. Over the following decades, there were, indeed, fewer and fewer attacks by Native Americans. It should be noted that the local Native American population dropped during those years, reducing the potential for conflict. Native Americans simply did not have adequate numbers of warriors to attack an ever-increasing number of Virginia settlers who continued to arrive in the colony by the thousands. Whether the wall at Middle Plantation itself had much to do with the diminishing uprisings is difficult to determine. But its presence undoubtedly caused a new generation of Virginians to feel safer on the colonial frontier.

4

The Making of Middle Plantation

Middle Plantation was founded, then, in 1633 as an outpost settlement to defend the main colony at Jamestown from attack. Unfortunately, through midcentury, it remained Middle Plantation's only claim to fame. It was during the second half of the 1600s that Middle Plantation would become less known for its fortified wall and more for its increasing number of local settlers, including planters who relied on tobacco cultivation for their livelihood. Over the last 50 years of the century, the region lured greater numbers of wealthy planters "who recognized good land for their homes and tobacco fields."[26]

IMPORTANT PLANTERS

One of the first planters to establish himself at Middle Plantation during the last half of the 1600s was John Page. He reached Virginia in 1650. First, he settled in Gloucester County, but soon moved to York County and the Middle Plantation region. By 1662, the prospering planter had overseen the construction of a large brick house for his family, which included his wife and

With his arrival in Virginia in 1650, John Page became one of the first planters to establish himself at Middle Plantation. Many credit Page as the founding father of Williamsburg, because the settlement's buildings, including the Wren Building, were patterned after structures that he built.

children. He was also making a name for himself in the growing settlement town. Page became involved in colonial politics and government, holding a series of public offices. Elected as high sheriff of York County in 1677, he was serving as a member of

---

MANSIONS IN THE WILDERNESS

Throughout its early decades, Virginia's Middle Plantation did not manage to attract many settlers. The region was noted for little but its defensive wall, intended to keep Native Americans and English settlers apart. But by the mid-seventeenth century, more and more colonists arrived, establishing extensive tobacco plantations and accumulating personal wealth. This wealth led some planters to build homes to match their prosperity. Among those who led the way in elaborate home construction were the Ludwells and John Page.

The Ludwell brothers eventually built a fabulous home called Rich Neck, which would serve as "the largest, most luxurious private home in Virginia"* with the exception of Governor Berkeley's house, Green Spring, a mansion that stood in James City County. The Ludwell's Rich Neck included a pair of brick houses "with elegant details, such as expansive delft tiles surrounding the fireplaces."** These houses, as well as Page's house, were capped with roofing tiles, which was rare in Virginia at the time.

These important planter homes stood out among the other homes in the Middle Plantation region. The larger number of local planters built smaller, less substantial homes. Modern archaeology has unearthed many such homes in the Tidewater region. The vast majority fall into a category of house based on post-in-the-ground construction. Many such houses were quite simple wooden homes having no sills to provide platforms for floorboards. Perhaps surprising to many people today is the fact that several Virginia planters, even those who were wealthy, lived in smallish houses sheathed with clapboard (boards that run horizontally and overlap one another top to bottom). Many such homes had only dirt floors, as well.

For this reason, the substantial and elaborate brick homes of John Page and the Ludwell brothers stood out even more.

---

* Robert P. Maccubbin, ed., *Williamsburg, Virginia: A City before the State, 1699–1999* (Published by the City of Williamsburg, 2000), 18.

** Ibid.

the governor's council by the 1680s. By then, the council was the second house of Virginia's colonial government, the first being the House of Burgesses. Page was also a civic leader, serving as a member of the local Bruton Parish Church vestry.

Middle Plantation would become home to other influential colonists, including James Bray and Otho Thorpe. Both would be members of the governor's council during the third quarter of the 1600s. Just a few years after John Page's arrival at Middle Plantation, Thomas Ludwell immigrated to Virginia as the colony's newly appointed secretary. He, too, took land at Middle Plantation, establishing his tobacco lands at the headwaters of Archer's Hope Creek. He convinced a brother, Philip, to come live at Middle Plantation with him. The Ludwell brothers were close neighbors to John Page.

These three men—John Page and Thomas and Philip Ludwell—would have a dramatic impact on Middle Plantation's development and progress. They became wealthy leaders in the region. The Ludwell's plantation became quite prosperous. There can be no doubt that these three men were among the most important residents in Middle Plantation:

> Like Page, the Ludwells were men on the make in the new colony, eager to reap the rewards that government service offered in Virginia. While their plantation was more distant from the core of Middle Plantation's settlement than was Page's, they also served as vestrymen for Bruton Parish, which was named in honor of the English town that the Ludwells had called home.[27]

With men such as Page, the Ludwells, Bray, and Thorpe, Middle Plantation eventually gained a more favorable reputation. By 1676, the settlement was "considered a place of importance by men in the colony."[28] The town was considered by many to be "the very Heart and Centre of the Country,"[29] even though Jamestown was still the governmental seat and capital and home to Governor Berkeley.

Bacon's Rebellion would bring a greater level of importance to Middle Plantation. The 1676 revolt brought Bacon to Middle Plantation that summer. It was in the frontier town that Bacon compiled his declaration against Governor Berkeley and his councilors. This meant that the Virginia revolutionary's document "listed grievances against the powerful men in the colony, including John Page, the Ludwells, and Page's neighbor Otho Thorpe."[30]

Throughout the days of Bacon's Rebellion, the town and lands of Middle Plantation remained important to the unfolding drama. When Berkeley fled Jamestown, which was later burned by Bacon and his men, he first went to the Eastern Shore of Virginia, only to later take up residence at Middle Plantation. (His own home, Green Spring, was plundered by Bacon's men.) At Middle Plantation, Berkeley was the guest of the aforementioned James Bray, and later stayed at the home of John Page. It was at Middle Plantation that Governor Berkeley ordered the execution of one of Bacon's rebel "lieutenants," William Drummond.

A MOVE TO MIDDLE PLANTATION

With Jamestown destroyed by Bacon's followers, the Virginia government was forced to take up residence elsewhere. Middle Plantation, the colony's second-most important settlement, seemed the logical choice. While the members of the House of Burgesses met in several places in the years after Bacon's failed rebellion, Middle Plantation was one of the most important. The burgesses met at Otho Thorpe's home in October 1677. The governor's council met there in 1682 and 1690. On two separate occasions, in 1677 and again in 1680, special ceremonial meetings were held at Middle Plantation between various Native American sachems, or leaders, and colony officials.

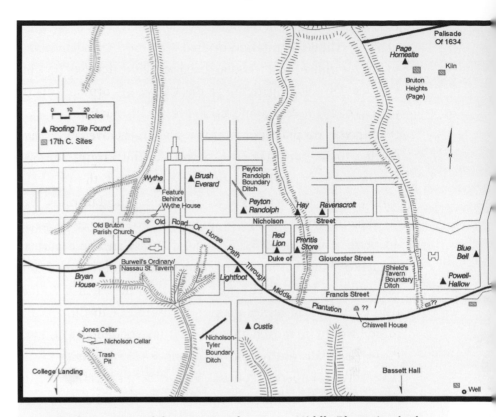

By the last quarter of the seventeenth century, Middle Plantation had become an important meeting place for the House of Burgesses. This map depicts the horse path that connected Jamestown and Yorktown and the many brick structures that had been built in Middle Plantation by the 1690s.

Another Native American conference took place there with the governor in 1698.

Each of these meetings reminded those who held important positions, such as burgesses and councilors, that Middle Plantation was a good location for official Virginia business. After all, for men like John Page and others, this move meant that meetings were held much closer to their homes and plantations. It would be Page who would mount an organized effort to have the official capital of Virginia Colony permanently located at Middle Plantation, taking up the cause as early as

1677, just after the end of Bacon's Rebellion. He and other residents of Middle Plantation drafted a petition and delivered it to the commissioners who had been sent to the colony by King Charles II to investigate the causes of Bacon's uprising. Their plea: to have the capital moved to Middle Plantation.

But the royal inspectors were not much interested, continuing to feel that Jamestown was the only viable location for the colony's capital, because it was situated on one of the colony's most important rivers, the James. As the commissioners explained things, moving the capital would make no sense. To them, it would be the same as if "Middlesex [a region in England] should have desired, that London might have beene new built on Highgat Hill, and removed from the grand River [the Thames] that brings them in their Trade."[31] If the colonial capital was to be moved, it would not take place in 1677. Even most Virginians did not favor the move. The majority would have agreed with one colonist who described Jamestown as the "most ancient and convenient place"[32] for the capital to be located. Perhaps just as important, many of the colony's public officers and political figures held property in and around Jamestown, not Middle Plantation.

But Middle Plantation's future was poised for change regardless. Bacon's Rebellion had not only managed to destroy Jamestown, it also caused English officials in London to rethink the social order in Virginia. Before the rebellion was defeated, King Charles II had decided to send 1,000 English troops to Virginia to put down the uprising by force. Unfortunately, these forces arrived in Virginia too late to have an impact on the civil revolt. But they remained in the colony for several years after. This large number of troops would be stationed at Middle Plantation. They were barracked near the town, and an accompanying powder magazine was built to house weapons and gunpowder. The people welcomed the arrival of these troops, and some of the town's leading citizens organized food collections to help feed the soldiers. Early in 1677, the House of Burgesses passed an act that authorized the troops to use a large plot of land near Middle Plantation, where they could plant some food crops, especially corn. The future of Virginia was turning away from Jamestown. Its focus would, over the following two decades, continue to revolve around Middle Plantation.

5

A Governor's Contribution

Even though Jamestown was burned in 1677, the decision to move the colonial capital of Virginia from the colony's original settlement to another did not take place overnight. Throughout the following 15 years, events redirected the center of Virginia's civic life from Jamestown to Williamsburg, which was originally known as Middle Plantation. During the 20 years following Bacon's uprising, Middle Plantation continued to make great strides in its growth and development. By 1683, its religious center, Bruton Parish Church, was rebuilt. A new worship center was constructed, "large and grandly designed to match [Middle Plantation's] impressive and attractive homes."[33] The members of the church's vestry made important donations in support of the project, especially John Page, who offered "to give lande sufficient for the Church and Church Yard."[34]

The move of the capital from Jamestown to Middle Plantation was due to the actions of several men who played key roles in transferring the importance of Virginia's colonial

Following the removal of Governor William Berkeley in 1677, Lord Thomas Culpeper was appointed Virginia's new governor. For the first three years of his governorship, Culpeper ruled Virginia through his deputies, but when he finally did arrive in 1680, he gained popularity by pardoning those who had participated in Bacon's Rebellion.

capital from Jamestown to Williamsburg. Perhaps most important among them was Francis Nicholson, who was appointed lieutenant governor in 1690.

Following Bacon's Rebellion, King Charles II sent his group of royal inspectors to Virginia to investigate what had happened between Governor Berkeley and his colonists that had caused the revolt in the first place. The still-powerful Berkeley would not cooperate with the king's commissioners and months passed before they were able to wrest power from him. But the years that immediately followed did not bring stability to Jamestown specifically or Virginia generally. A new governor, Lord Culpeper, was appointed, but he did not sail to Virginia immediately and only took his place in the colony in 1680, after Charles II threatened to remove him. Even then, he only remained in Virginia for four months, then returned to England. He paid Virginia a second call in 1682, then left the colony again, never to return. It appears the idea of being Virginia's governor appealed to Culpeper more than actually being governor.

Lord Culpeper was replaced by yet another governor—Lord Howard of Effingham—who "was more conscientious but also a harder man all around."[35] Just as Berkeley had staked a claim of greater power over Virginia, Governor Howard did the same. For the colonists in Jamestown and those scattered up and down Virginia's rivers, these were difficult times:

> For Virginia all this meant years of tyranny and disorder and poverty. In the 1670's and 1680's, the Assembly was systematically stripped of many previously granted rights: the right to hear judicial appeals, the right to elect their own clerk [so the governor's "spy" might be placed in the burgesses' midst], the right to control all revenues.[36]

Despite this difficult time in Virginia's history, a brighter future lay ahead. In 1685, Charles II died and was succeeded by his brother James II, a Roman Catholic, who was "a mulishly shortsighted man even by the standards of a family famed for obstinacy."[37] Just as his father, Charles I, had been removed from

In 1689, King William III and Queen Mary II forced King James II, Mary's father, from England and became joint sovereigns of the country. In 1693, the couple chartered the College of William and Mary, which is today the second-oldest institution of higher learning in the United States behind Harvard.

power by revolution during the 1640s, so James II would face a revolution of his own just three years after rising to the throne of England. Another revolt, often called the "Glorious Revolution" or "Bloodless Revolution," managed to remove James from power (unlike his father, Charles I, he was not killed, but wisely decided to give up his throne and accept exile in France) and replace him with his daughter Mary, a Protestant, and her husband, William Prince of Orange, who was already ruling the Netherlands. By the late 1680s, William and Mary were ruling England.

GOVERNOR NICHOLSON

The change of English monarchs would directly affect the history of Virginia. The king and queen ordered Lord Howard to return to England from the colony. They did not immediately remove him from his office, but by recalling him, they had removed a thorn from the side of the English colonists. In his place, the lieutenant governor, Francis Nicholson, was to run the colony.

He was a breath of fresh air to Virginia. Although he had a sometimes violent temper, he proved himself to be a capable administrator who was "genuinely interested in the people of Virginia."[38] He frequently conversed with those who lived in the commonwealth. He did not remain holed up in Jamestown, but visited the frontier settlements along the rivers, where he personally inspected colonial fortifications and defenses. He supported more schools in the colony and talked to many influential Virginians, often inviting them to dine with him at his governor's home, seeking their advice on how to improve life in the colony. Nicholson became more popular "with the sports-loving Virginians by instituting public athletic contests— although he confined these 'Olympic Games' to 'the better sort of Virginians only.'"[39] He gained even greater support from his subjects when he donated £150 of his own money for the establishment of Virginia's first college. That college would forever change the future of colonial Williamsburg.

THE FOUNDING OF VIRGINIA'S COLLEGE

Perhaps no single individual was more instrumental in ensuring that a college was established in Virginia's Middle Plantation than "an energetic Anglican clergyman,"[40] the colony's Reverend James Blair. The church leader had arrived in Virginia from England in 1685. He was an ordained minister of the Church of England, who had earned degrees at the University of Edinburgh in Scotland. Upon his arrival, Reverend Blair began to make a name for himself. He moved to Middle Plantation and established himself on land owned by the Ludwell brothers. Soon he married a Virginia girl, Sarah Harrison, whose father was an important and wealthy planter in Surry County. Blair and Governor Nicholson became close friends, and the minister was granted a seat on the governor's council. Blair was making things happen in Virginia. He would later be appointed by the Bishop of London as his commissary, or deputy, for the colony of Virginia. (Part of the Bishop's diocese included Virginia.)

In 1689, the Virginia House of Burgesses first took up discussions concerning the possibility of establishing a college in Virginia. And it was the learned Reverend Blair who became the biggest supporter for the establishment of that college. Through his political connections, he convinced fellow councilors and burgesses. By 1693, colonial leaders were ready to begin planning the college. There were those, however, who did not support the idea. Among them was the official who was responsible for the colony's money, Comptroller Sir Edward Seymour. He believed talk of a college to be a waste of time and money. He saw Virginia as a place occupied by frontiersmen and hardworking farmers and planters. What need did they have of a college? Virginia was dependent on tobacco production. Seymour and Reverend Blair did not agree on the need for a college in Virginia, but Blair reminded Seymour that a college would provide learned ministers for the colony. He told the hesitant comptroller: "The people of Virginia have souls to be saved as well as the people of England."[41] Even these words did not convince Seymour. "Souls!" he shouted at Reverend Blair. "Damn your souls! Make tobacco!"[42]

Despite Seymour's lack of imagination for the future of Virginians, plans for the college went forward. Wealthy colonists raised £2,000 in support of a college. Middle Plantation

STUDENTS ARGUE FOR MIDDLE PLANTATION

Reverend James Blair was undoubtedly the most important voice in the campaign to establish a college at Virginia's Middle Plantation, and he also used his influence when it came to moving the capital of Virginia from Jamestown to the same town site. Through his efforts, the move to Middle Plantation, now renamed Williamsburg, would become reality. Part of Blair's plan to convince the House of Burgesses to consider the move hinged on the efforts of five students from the newly opened College of William and Mary.

During the May Day celebrations held in 1699, the year following the fire that destroyed Jamestown's second statehouse, Reverend Blair arranged for five students to appear before the House of Burgesses to deliver speeches. Their purpose: to convince the burgesses to move the capital to Middle Plantation. All of the students had been carefully trained and coached on their subject by Reverend Blair. Their words were purposeful and to the point.

As one student spoke, he put forward the positive aspects of a capital at Middle Plantation, including naming the prominent men who already lived there, including some who were burgesses: "Here is good neighborhood of as many substantial Housekeepers that could give great help towards the supplying and maintaining of a constant Market."* He went on to describe the progress that had already taken place at Middle Plantation, including efforts "towards the beginning of a Town, a Church, an ordinary [a tavern], several stores, two Mills, a smiths shop, a Grammar School, and above all the College."**

Another student spoke about one of Middle Plantation's most important leaders, John Page. Page, the student reminded his listeners, had been extremely supportive of the opening of a college at Middle Plantation. Page planter and civic leader John Page even donated a portion of his own lands at Middle Plantation as a possible location for the planned institution of higher learning. The House of Burgesses drew up and approved a petition requesting a charter for a college. Virginia officials then sent Reverend Blair to London to meet with King William and Queen Mary.

was referred to as "the person that had the chief honour to be the first to move in procuring" a college.*** The William and Mary student's praise of Page was not idle flattery. The Honorable Colonel Page had been dead for seven years.

The students also presented specific arguments that had been put forward by many against moving the capital. One was the claim that the James River was a much better river connection to seagoing trading ships than the "two Creeks navigable only by small craft that draw 6 or 7 foot [of] water."† To counter that argument, one student claimed "the many other merits of location outweighed its inconvenient river access."††

Reverend Blair's conspiracy to convince the burgesses to authorize the capital move was persuasive. The students' May Day speeches managed to convince several burgesses of the need and value of such a move from Jamestown to Middle Plantation. The following month, on June 7, the assembly voted to build a new statehouse at the site where the College of William and Mary already stood.

---

* Harold B. Gill, Jr. and Ann Finlayson, *Colonial Virginia* (Nashville: Thomas Nelson, 1973), 81.

** Ibid.

*** Hugh Howard, *Colonial Houses: The Historic Homes of Williamsburg* (New York: Henry N. Abrams, 2004), 9.

† George Humphrey Yetter, *Williamsburg Before and After: The Rebirth of Virginia's Colonial Capital* (Williamsburg: The Colonial Williamsburg Foundation, 1988), 18–19.

†† Ibid., 19.

The royal monarchs were interested in helping establish a college in the New World. The Spanish, after all, had established universities long ago in their Latin American empire. William and Mary granted the requested charter and even appointed Reverend Blair as the college's first president. One important incentive to gaining the monarchs' approval was the offer to name the college after William and Mary. Blair returned to Virginia triumphant. The king and queen had granted an endowment of money to help finance the college, and Virginians began donating from their own wealth, as well. (The college endowment even received donations from several pirates who were being held by Virginia officials in prison. They hoped to gain their freedom by giving to the worthy cause.)

With the establishment of the College of William and Mary, Reverend Blair had found his lifelong calling. He remained the college's first president for the next half century, as well as the representative of the Bishop of London. He had an impact and input on nearly every aspect of the college, including "building construction, organization of the curriculum, and hiring of faculty."[43] The primary purpose of the college was to educate and train Christian ministers, providing them with studies in "letters and manners."[44] One of the key goals of the college program was to send ministers into the field to teach Christianity to the Native Americans. William and Mary's structure also provided for a grammar school where younger students studied Greek, Latin, reading, writing, and "vulgar Arithmatick."[45] Construction on the college's first permanent building was begun in 1695. It was a typically English brick building, described by one of the college's mathematics professors as one "first modeled by Sir Christopher Wren, [and] adapted to the nature of the country by the gentlemen there."[46] Wren was, perhaps, the most famous architect in all of London. The college opened its doors to students in 1698.

Famed English architect Sir Christopher Wren, who also designed London's St. Paul Cathedral, is said to have planned the College of William and Mary's first structure, the Wren Building. Wren is depicted in this portrait by Sir Godfrey Kneller at Wadham College in Oxford, England.

A SAD END TO JAMESTOWN

Perhaps nothing during the 1690s did more to encourage the movement of Virginia's governmental center from Jamestown to Middle Plantation than the organizing and opening of the

College of William and Mary, with the exception of yet another fire in Jamestown. Once again, this time on October 31, 1698, the Jamestown capitol building, known as the statehouse, burned down. Barely 20 years had passed since Bacon and his men had put Jamestown to the torch. While the old capitol had been rebuilt after Bacon's uprising, there were those who were convinced after the second fire that the capital should be moved.

A campaign was launched to move the capital of Virginia Colony to Middle Plantation. Governor Nicholson supported the move. Nicholson had only recently been appointed as Virginia's governor for a second time. He had been replaced by another royal appointee, Sir Edmund Andros, during the late 1690s, but Andros had proven extremely unpopular with many Virginians, including Reverend Blair.

During this period, Jamestown's prominence began to fade. For nearly a century, the town had been the important trade, social, and political center of Virginia Colony, since the days of its founding in 1607. But Jamestown had never been a popular site for colonization. Supporters of Middle Plantation spoke of its "dry and champaign land"[47] and its healthy environs. In addition, it was now the home of the College of William and Mary. Critics of the proposal argued that Middle Plantation had little to offer of substance. There were few people living there, and the site could only boast the college's Wren building, the Bruton Parish Church, and the cluttered remains of the old defensive wall that had been long forgotten. However, by 1699, the House of Burgesses passed "an Act directing the Building of the Capitoll and the City of Williamsburgh."[48] The burgesses thought it appropriate to name their new capital after King William. (Queen Mary had died several years earlier.) With the approach of a new century, the planned town of Williamsburg would soon be enjoying its season in the sun.

6

The Planning of Williamsburg

The former site of Middle Plantation, now having been re-named Williamsburg, would witness extraordinary changes during the immediate years to follow. While Jamestown had been abandoned, Middle Plantation had not been chosen for what it was so much as *for what it would become.* To that end, Governor Nicholson led the way in planning his new capital. Between his terms as Virginia's governor, he had served as Maryland's governor and had helped lay out the town plan for Annapolis, Maryland's new capital. His work would be extremely specific and include decisions concerning many of Williamsburg's details. One Virginia burgess, Robert Beverley, would later write about Nicholson's involvement in organizing the town plan. Nicholson, he wrote, "mark'd out the street in many places, so that they might represent the figure of a W, in memory of his late majesty King William, after whose name the town was call'd Williamsburg."[49] This particular idea was later either changed or scrapped, in part, because of the lay of the land where Williamsburg would be built. The town would instead follow the natural topography of short valleys and small, rolling hills.

NICHOLSON'S DESIGNS

Governor Nicholson did not work alone on organizing the layout for the new town. He employed a surveyor, Theodorick Bland, to carry out a survey and establish a boundary line for the new Williamsburg. Bland's survey would include 220 acres of what formerly was Middle Plantation property. Because some buildings already existed, the new survey was partially based on the positions of such places as Bruton Parish Church. Bland divided the new capital into two districts. One would center on the 160 acres around the church and the college, which were identified as the residential community. The other 60 acres along the eastern end of the town would be the sites for the government and administration of the new capital, as well as the location for the businesses, shops, stores, and taverns. The survey also established the routes to Williamsburg's ports, which would connect to both the James and York rivers. Today, these routes are South Henry Street and Capitol Landing Road.

How the new town would be laid out had already, in part, been decided by the very act passed by the colonial Assembly. That ordinance, "an early instance of city planning in America,"[50] had ordered the grounds of the new town subdivided into half-acre lots. With a house lot of that size, there would be plenty of room for private gardens and orchards. Many of these lots would be placed on either side of a main street that would run nearly a mile in length. It would stretch eastward from the College of William and Mary's Wren Building to the new statehouse, which would always be referred to as "The Capitol." Just as Williamsburg was named for King William, this new street would be named Duke of Gloucester Street, after the son of Princess Anne, who would one day inherit the throne from her father. It was to be a splendid road through the town, measuring 99 feet in width. Two additional streets would parallel the main road from the college to the capitol, both named for Governor Francis Nicholson—Francis Street would be

Built between 1695 and 1699, the Sir Christopher Wren Building on the campus of the College of William and Mary is the oldest academic building in continuous use in the United States. Today, the building houses classrooms and faculty offices.

located south of Duke of Gloucester Street, and Nicholson Street would lie to the north. Each house built along these three main thoroughfares had to meet certain specifications. These dwellings also had to be set back a specified distance from the street itself.

With the establishment of the new capital at Williamsburg, hundreds of Virginians soon made the planned town their home. Williamsburg became a showcase throughout its first generation for new styles of architecture, both for public buildings and private ones. The construction of edifices and dwellings with "great hipped roofs, broken by dormers, tall, slender chimneys, clock towers and cupolas"[51] made the colonial capital unique. (Cupolas are usually short, center towers that adorn the roofs of churches and public buildings, as well as larger private homes.)

There was wealth behind many of the houses built in the new town with, as described by Robert Beverley, "their Stories much higher than formerly, and their Windows large, and Sasht with Cristal Glass."[52] Modern historians estimate that, among Williamsburg's 2,000 permanent inhabitants, approximately 15 percent were "members of the professional or gentry class of the town—the lawyers, doctors, clergymen, college instructors, and the wealthy planters who served as members of the Governor's Council."[53] Approximately one of every two heads of household were from the class known as the "middling sort," which included the most important artisans, craftsmen, and merchants. Below them was the "lower sort," a group that included apprentices, tavern keepers, manual laborers, and smalltime shopkeepers and craftsmen. But of all of Williamsburg's social classes, approximately half were black slaves.

Most of the simpler houses in Williamsburg were sided with clapboard. But brick was used on several buildings, including the Capitol Building, the courthouse, jail (the British spelling is gaol), and the Governor's Palace. When brick was utilized, it was laid in a pattern known as the Flemish bond, which consists of placing bricks lengthwise and endwise, then repeating. The majority of the homes in colonial Williamsburg were one story, with some space available in attics for sleeping.

Because fire had destroyed Jamestown more than once, the Capitol Building at Williamsburg was built with no fireplaces. Even candles and smoking pipes were not allowed inside! In time, with the memory of Jamestown's burned-out statehouse forgotten, fireplaces were later added to the Capitol Building. Fire did destroy the capitol in January 1747, but the building was rebuilt by 1753.

A NEW GOVERNOR FOR NEW WILLIAMSBURG

The early days of Williamsburg's founding and growth were exciting times of progress and change, both in the colony and back in England. King William III would not remain the English monarch for long after 1699. In 1702, he suffered an accident when he fell from a horse. The shock of the fall resulted in his death. His daughter, Princess Anne, took her place on the throne. Within two years, her son, the Duke of Gloucester, died of scarlet fever.

Back in Williamsburg, work on the new colonial capital was progressing. A Swiss immigrant, Francis Louis Michel, visited Williamsburg in 1702. He had arrived recently in Virginia to make plans for founding another Virginia town, one to serve as a haven for some of his fellow Swiss. Using Williamsburg as his inspiration, Michel drew sketches of the buildings and the layout of the town streets. He later wrote about what he had seen in Williamsburg: "It is a large place, where a city is intended and staked out to be built. . . . More buildings will be built year after year."[54] In his report, he noted that the colonial settlement included the Bruton Parish Church, the college's Wren Building, a new capitol building that was not yet completed, as well as several "stores, gentlemen's houses, and eight ordinaries, or inns."[55]

Governor Francis Nicholson left his mark on early Williamsburg as few men in Virginia could or did. But he, too, would not remain in power for long. The middle-aged Nicholson seems to have fallen in love with a much younger Virginia girl, who did not return his interest. Having been spurned, the governor appears to have become emotionally and mentally unbalanced. Nicholson's violent temper became even greater and more erratic. At the same time, he and Reverend Blair began to quarrel with one another. The result was that Blair managed to get

Governor Nicholson recalled in 1704. Williamsburg was barely five years old at that time.

The colony of Virginia then experienced a succession of three governors whose terms were short and unimportant, all within a six-year period. During that period, in 1705, a fire broke out in the College of William and Mary's Wren Building, leaving it a burned-out brick shell. This would be the first of several fires that would plague Williamsburg throughout the 1700s. With its main building destroyed, college officials debated whether to rebuild on the same site or select another and start over. By 1709, the decision was made to build on the site of the old building, incorporating as much of the earlier walls as were structurally sound. But the new college building would be a bit different than the original. One of the changes was that the college building's third story would include a series of long rows of dormer windows that stood up along the roofline.

A SCOTTISH GOVERNOR

By 1710, the people of Williamsburg saw yet another governor arrive, one who would leave an enduring legacy on the colonial capital and Virginia, as well. He was a Scotsman named Alexander Spotswood. He came from an influential family; many of his relatives had served in either the military or the clergy. Alexander's great-great-grandfather, the Archbishop of St. Andrews, had crowned James VI, the Scottish king, as the English monarch James I. Alexander's father had been an army surgeon. The young Spotswood followed in his father's footsteps, entering the army when he was 17 years old, and serving in the Earl of Bath's infantry regiment. When he left the army, Spotswood had achieved the rank of lieutenant colonel. By then, he was the Duke of Marlborough's assistant quartermaster general. He saw action during Queen Anne's War and was wounded. It was at the end of that conflict that he was appointed governor of the

In 1710, Alexander Spotswood was appointed lieutenant governor of Virginia. Like his predecessor, Francis Nicholson, Spotswood left his mark on Williamsburg; he oversaw the construction of many of the town's buildings, including a powder magazine to store the local militia's gunpowder.

Commonwealth of Virginia at the age of 34. Spotswood was actually the colony's lieutenant governor; the true governor held the title and remained in England.

Spotswood proved to be extremely popular with the people of Virginia. As he would himself write, "I have a fair prospect of a good Agreement with the People & believe I shall live very contentedly here."[56] The new governor would take to his new office and its duties with great energy and imagination. Just as Nicholson had left his mark early in the development of

GOVERNOR SPOTSWOOD AND BLACKBEARD

While Governor Spotswood proved himself to be a capable public leader, administrator, and even architect, he is credited with improving Virginia in at least one other way—battling pirates. This would require him to challenge one of the most famous pirates ever to ply the high seas of the New World, the notorious Blackbeard.

The years of Queen Anne's War (1702–13) pitted the English and the French against one another. To aid in its efforts, the Crown granted English pirates letters of marque. These letters gave written authority to these men to operate at sea as privateers, those in their own service who would attack French merchant ships and steal their cargoes, all in the name of the queen. When the war ended in 1713, the letters of marque were no longer in effect. However, this only meant that those who had simply been pirates before the war returned to being pirates again—and outlaws, as well.

Such pirates sailed the waters along the Atlantic seaboard and preyed on any ships they considered vulnerable prizes. Their presence proved a challenge to such colonial authorities as Governor Spotswood. Earlier Virginia governors had faced the same problems with pirates. In 1700, Governor Nicholson launched an expedition against a pirate ship that plied the waters of Chesapeake Bay. The governor himself fought in this 10-hour sea battle that resulted in the capture of the pirate vessel, along with its crew of 60 men. Virginia's collector of customs was killed during the battle, falling at the governor's side.

In 1717, Governor Spotswood appealed to officials in England: "Our Capes have been for these six Weeks pass'd in a manner blocked up by those pyrates, and diverse Ships inward bound, taken and plundered by them."* Soon, a British man-of-war, a large navy vessel, was dispatched to Virginia to deal with the pirate problem. But the ship was in such poor condition that it was unable to launch an attack against any pirate ship in the region.

The most successful pirate plaguing Virginia at that time was Edward Teach, who was known as Blackbeard. He gained his nickname through "his habit of flaunting his long beard by wearing it in sausage curls or pigtails tied with ribbon."** Teach operated out of North Carolina, where he may have

Williamsburg, so too would Governor Spotswood. One of his first endeavors was the addition of the Palace Green to the still-developing town layout plan. Then, he turned his imagination to the old Bruton Parish Church. Spotswood was even asked by

bribed the colonial governor there with 60 barrels of sugar to leave him alone. From his base, Blackbeard and his men raided ships constantly and even terrorized planters along various Tidewater rivers. Governor Spotswood soon concentrated his efforts at stopping Blackbeard.

Using his own money, the governor hired out two sloops, manning them from the crews of two navy frigates docked in Virginia. The sloops were placed under the command of First Lieutenant Robert Maynard. Maynard sailed to North Carolina in search of Blackbeard. He did not have to search for long. Setting out on November 17, 1718, the sloops spotted Blackbeard's ship within five days. A sea battle ensued, resulting in Teach and several of his men boarding one of the sloops. British sailors and Blackbeard's pirates fought across the deck of Maynard's ship in hand-to-hand combat, "till the Sea was tinctur'd with Blood round the Vessel."[***] During the battle, with swords and cutlasses ringing against one another, Blackbeard and Maynard fought one another directly. It was a fight that Edward Teach would lose, the dreaded pirate falling dead on the ship's deck, his body bleeding from 20 sword wounds and 5 bullet holes. After the sailors from the second sloop boarded Teach's ship, *Adventure*, another fight ensued. The pirates lost both shipboard fights. Nearly two dozen of Blackbeard's men died in these sword battles. Among the British sailors, casualties included 10 killed and another 24 wounded. Maynard returned to Virginia with the head of Blackbeard the Pirate hanging from the bowsprit of his ship, still sporting its trademark ribbons.

An additional 15 pirates, taken prisoner by Maynard and his men, were subsequently tried and ordered executed by hanging. All this pleased Governor Spotswood, of course, but turned him into one of the most hated royal officials in the British colonies, at least as far as the region's pirates were concerned.

---

 * Harold B. Gill, Jr. and Ann Finlayson, *Colonial Virginia* (Nashville: Thomas Nelson), 85.
 ** Ibid.
 *** Ibid., 86.

the people of the town to design a new church himself. He also designed a new powder magazine (warehouse) for storing the local militia's gunpowder.

All this was work for which Spotswood was well suited. As he was later described in 1715 by a visiting aristocrat, the governor was

> well acquainted with Figures, and so good a mathematician, that his Skill in Architecture, and in the laying out of Ground to the Best Advantage, is yet to be seen in Virginia, by the Building of an elegant safe magazine, in the Centre of Williamsburgh, and in the considerable Improvements which he made to the Governor's House and Gardens.[57]

In addition to the new church design and the new powder magazine, with its eight-sided design and tall roof, Spotswood increased the size of the Williamsburg jail and helped create the layout for the executive mansion, the Governor's Palace. He was able to have a significant impact on the building's design, because progress on the mansion was so slow. While colonial officials nearly rushed to rebuild a new capitol building after the Jamestown statehouse burned in 1698, it was "not shared when discussing how to house the governor."[58] It was not until 1706 that the initial steps were taken to begin work on the structure.

That year, the colonial assembly allotted £3,000 for the erecting of a two-story, brick mansion to be built two blocks north of the Bruton Parish Church on Palace Street. The palace was to measure 54 by 48 feet "with sash windows, a vaulted space and other rooms in the cellar, slate roof, and detached kitchen and stable."[59] But progress on the palace proved slow and disappointing. By 1709, the building was not yet completed and the money earmarked for its construction had all been spent. When Virginia lawmakers balked at authorizing

During his term as lieutenant governor, Alexander Spotswood was instrumental in helping design the layout of Virginia's governor's mansion. Although work began on the building in 1706, it was not completed until 1722, the same year Spotswood's term ended.

money for the mansion, the governor did not mince words, telling them: "This is a Matter in which Your Own Honour is . . . engaged."[60]

Ultimately, the work on the Governor's Palace dragged on for 14 years before the mansion was completed. It would become a masterpiece of public building in the New World. Spotswood's contributions to its completion were recognized by many, including an English professor at the College of William and Mary, who stated: "A magnificent structure, built at the publick expense, finished and beautified with gates, fine gardens, offices, walks, a fine canal, orchards, etc. with a great number of the best arms nicely posited by the ingenious contrivance of the most accomplished Colonel Spotswood."[61]

7

A City
Takes Shape

Within the first generation of settlement, Williamsburg had
already taken shape and had developed into a prosperous community. Governors Nicholson and Spotswood had left their
marks and helped to define the layout of the town with great
skill and forethought. The result was the establishment of a
tidy, well-designed urban landscape, which also served as the
colony's political center. The town was laid out with Duke of
Gloucester, Nicholson, and Francis streets all running east and
west, while intersecting thoroughfares ran north and south,
including Boundary, which ran in front of the college's Wren
Building, Henry, Nassau, England, Queen, Botetourt, and
Waller streets. While Duke of Gloucester Street was the great,
wide avenue running east and west, the street running north
and south in front of the Governor's Palace was also a magnificent thoroughfare. At the intersection of England Street and
Duke of Gloucester Street stood the town's courthouse. In front
of the courthouse was Market Square, a large open area located almost exactly in the center of the town. It was there that

Governor Spotswood had ordered the construction of the powder magazine in 1715.

Market Square was a focal point for the residents of Williamsburg. The square "served as a town common where markets and fairs were held regularly."[62] Just west of Market Square was Bruton Parish Church, which had been newly replaced in 1715, again with Governor Spotswood's involvement. The square served as Williamsburg's "civic open space."[63] It was flanked by Nicholson Street on its north side, Francis to the south, and on the east by Queen Street. Duke of Gloucester Street ran through its middle. This important square would be the site of many of the town's "commercial, military, and county legal affairs, as well as the scene of auctions, slave sales, and meetings."[64] It was also where the town's public water pump was located. On two occasions annually—April 23 (St. George's Day) and December 12—Market Square hosted an official town fair. Farmers would come in from the outlying lands and sell livestock, as well as a variety of other goods. It was a wild time of buying and selling, punctuated by "games, cudgeling matches, cockfights, and a chase for 'A Pig, with the Tail soap'd.'"[65]

A PERIOD OF RAPID GROWTH

For those who called Williamsburg home, the colonial town was an impressive site. In its earliest years, the center of the community had been the College of William and Mary. Then, the outpost of studies and academics was given a boost by the movement of the capital and the governor to the town. Williamsburg was changed into a town of politics, dominated by the capitol. But there were other influences on its growth and importance. Meetings of the General Court were held there eventually, as well as the Governor's Council and the General Assembly of the colonial legislature. (Residents referred to the days when the court was in session in Williamsburg as "Publick Times."

The courthouse that stands today was built in the early 1770s. Two earlier courthouses preceded it.) These additions brought new people to town and new businesses as well. People needed places to eat and sleep and gather together for conversation. Taverns and inns opened their doors for business. There were law offices, shops, blacksmiths, and stables. These served not only the permanent residents of the town, but those who lived in Williamsburg only during certain times of the year, such as members of the House of Burgesses who came and went with the opening and closing of each season's session.

One of the earliest taverns built in Williamsburg was the Raleigh Tavern. Opened in 1717, the Raleigh was one of the

BLACK LABORERS CONTRIBUTE TO WILLIAMSBURG

Among those who labored on the buildings at Williamsburg, whether public or private, were black workers, both slave and free. Blacks were first brought to Virginia in 1619, just 12 years after the founding of Jamestown. When these first Africans were delivered to the colonial community, slavery did not exist in Virginia. These early black arrivals were not considered slaves, but workers, not much different from white worker immigrants, most of whom were indentured servants. Such workers came to America as poor immigrants who could not afford to pay their own passage to the New World. Someone else paid their ship's passage and these workers were then "indentured" to that person, which required them to work off their debt, usually through seven years of labor. When the indenture was completed, the servant was granted his or her "freedom dues," which might include a new suit of clothes, some farming tools, and seed, as well as his/her freedom, of course. For several decades following 1619, blacks brought from Africa were treated as temporary workers, then given their freedom.

In time, however, legally defined slavery created a system of forced labor for blacks, one that was indefinite. The British began buying black natives directly from Africa rather than importing them through another country, such as Holland or Spain. These imported workers were considered slaves as early as the mid-seventeenth century. Slave ships delivered their human cargoes up the James and York rivers, as well as at Hampton Roads.

town's most important unofficial gathering places, "a center for social, commercial, and political gatherings, small private and large public dinners, lectures and exhibits, and auctions of merchandise, property, and slaves."[66] Its ballroom—the Apollo Room—was "second in elegance only . . . [to] the Governor's Palace."[67] Through its grand years of the 1700s and early 1800s, Raleigh Tavern would host such Virginia notables as Patrick Henry, Thomas Jefferson, and George Washington, who made frequent references in his personal diary that he had "dined at the Raleigh."[68] There would be other taverns in colonial Williamsburg, including Wetherburn's Tavern, which first opened in 1743, and another that opened just two years after the Raleigh

The development of slavery in the British colonies, such as Virginia, meant that planters did not have to replace their workforce after only a few years. Once they "purchased" a black worker, he or she remained a slave for life. Such slaves eventually replaced the need for indentured white servants.

From the 1640s through the end of the century, Virginia law helped create and encourage a number of slave practices. Sometimes these laws overlapped and even conflicted. In 1705, the Virginia Assembly, including the House of Burgesses and the Governor's Council, met in colonial Williamsburg to pass new laws regarding enslaved Africans, free blacks, and the few Native Americans who were still living in Virginia. These changes and new laws were referred to as the 1705 Slave Code. The laws defined who slaves were, how they could and should be treated, what restrictions they would live under, and how they could be legally punished.

Whites in Virginia believed such laws were necessary given that so many slaves lived in the colony and because of the contributions that slaves were making as a labor force in the colony. Within the next 50 years, blacks in Virginia (the vast majority of whom were slaves) accounted for two of every five persons (40 percent) in the colony. Most of them were living in the Chesapeake region of Virginia, which included Williamsburg. In the colonial capital and the surrounding region, in fact, the black population may have even been as high as 50 percent.

Like its two predecessors, Williamsburg's third courthouse was centrally located in the town's Market Square. Constructed in 1770–71, the building's unique design includes an octagonal wooden cupola.

(it would later be known as the John Crump House), but the Raleigh would remain the most important street-level meeting place in Williamsburg throughout the 1700s.

The town of colonial Williamsburg grew rapidly during its first decades as Virginia's capital. It had grown so much that, by 1722, yet another English monarch, King George I, declared that Williamsburg should be considered a city. The community by then numbered close to 2,000 and there were more than 200 houses lining its well-delineated streets. The colonies boasted larger communities at that time, including New York City, Philadelphia, and Boston. And, despite Williamsburg's early

Opened in 1717, Raleigh Tavern soon became the central meeting place for Williamsburg's prominent residents. Revolutionary leaders such as Patrick Henry, Thomas Jefferson, and George Washington often frequented the Raleigh whenever they visited Williamsburg.

growth, which continued throughout the first half of the eighteenth century, the colonial center would never become a great American city. It had a unique style and well-designed layout. But colonial Williamsburg would forever remain of regional importance only.

WILLIAMSBURG'S SEASON IN THE SUN

The city of Williamsburg experienced its years of greatest importance and colonial power in the decades just before and after 1750. Much of its significance was centered on the work being done by the Governor's Councilors, the burgesses, and the meetings of the General Court, all of which met in the Capitol Building. The General Court and the House of Burgesses

Williamsburg's capitol was rebuilt in 1753 after fire destroyed the original building in 1747. Over the years, the Capitol Building was home to Virginia's legislative assembly, the House of Burgesses, and both Patrick Henry and Thomas Jefferson were sworn in as governor here.

both met on the first floor on opposite wings of the H-shaped building, while the council chamber was situated on the second floor, just above the General Court. Each played its role as an arm of Virginia government. The council was composed of a dozen men, all of whom were chosen for their importance to the colony. Most of them were wealthy planters. Those serving as burgesses were elected directly by the people, two from each of the counties, and one representing Jamestown, Norfolk, and Williamsburg. One burgess was even chosen to represent the College of William and Mary.

During nearly any era of Virginia's colonial history, the most important political figure was the governor. He was, after all, the direct and chosen representative of the British monarch. He had significant powers, including the ability to call sessions of the House of Burgesses, as well as to dissolve the body. The governor selected those who served as his councilors. Together, the governor and councilors sat as the General Court. This resulted in an overlap of power between the executive branch of government (the governor and councilors) and the judiciary (the General Court). The General Court was the colony's highest court. Any appeal of a decision issued by a lower court had to be decided by the General Court. Some cases, those that might result in a defendant losing his life or limb, originated in the General Court. For more than 40 years, the Capitol Building was the seat of a bustling community and a prospering colony, one of the most important among all the British colonies hugging the Atlantic coast.

In 1747, a tragic chapter in the capitol's history took place. A fire broke out early on the morning of January 30 of that year. Although the reason for the fire remained a mystery, the grand brick building was gutted. There were a few rumors of arson. During the discussions that followed concerning the rebuilding of the capitol, some burgesses favored moving the seat of Virginia government yet again. But, by a narrow margin of 40 to 38, the burgesses elected to rebuild the Capitol Building in Williamsburg. The work began in 1751 and was finished in 1753.

WILLIAMSBURG AND WAR

During the early 1750s, yet another war broke out between the French and the British in North America. This latest conflict, called the French and Indian War, came about, in part, because of events that took place in Williamsburg. One of the reasons for the conflict was the movement of the French from

Canada south into the frontier region known then as the Ohio Country, the lands south of the Great Lakes and north of the Ohio River. In 1753, Virginia governor Robert Dinwiddie sent a young militia officer into the Ohio Country to warn the French to leave the region. That officer was 21-year-old George Washington. Young Washington left Williamsburg on October 31, 1753, to deliver the message from the governor in the spring. The French did not agree to leave the region and, by the following year, the war had begun.

That spring, the House of Burgesses met in the capitol and voted for monies to raise a regiment of 300 militia troops. These troops were sent into the Ohio Country to counter the French threat. Washington was appointed as second in command, holding the rank of lieutenant colonel. The fighting soon unfolded along the frontier and continued for the next several years. By 1759, before the war was over, Washington had distinguished himself enough through his efforts that the House of Burgesses called him to one of their sessions to thank him for his services. In just a few more years, the British and their colonial allies would win the French and Indian War.

The decade of the 1760s fell between the events of the French and British conflict and the opening of the Revolutionary War. This was, perhaps, one of Williamsburg's greatest decades. The city hit its stride, reaching its peak of importance and population. Most of the town was still situated as it had been laid out more than half a century earlier. City life had extended out and beyond the original plan for the town by then. Although the Wren Building and the Capitol Building had served as bookends at either end of Duke of Gloucester Street, by the 1760s, one could walk beyond the capitol to a public space called the Exchange, "where planters squared accounts with one another, consigned tobacco to factors and sea captains, and arranged to purchase [slaves]."[69] There was an establishment called the Coffee House, which

young Thomas Jefferson, a law student in Williamsburg during the mid-1760s, liked to frequent, and the Williamsburg
theater. (Jefferson and George Washington were both fans of
the local performances.) Nearby were the public hanging gallows, where the convicted were executed when the General
Court was in session. This neighborhood also included the local horse racecourse, where racing and betting were common
pastimes for many.

Williamsburg's 2,000 or so permanent residents lived in approximately 300 houses, including the neighboring plantations.
But the city's population increased two times annually—fall and
spring—during Publick Times, when the courts were in session
and the assembly was meeting. At those times, Williamsburg
was crowded with two or three times its normal population. Fa-
vorite taverns, such as the Raleigh, Wetherburn's, and the King's
Arms were busy each day and evening until closing. Hous-
ing and lodging became scarce with inns and boardinghouses
"filled to overflowing" with as many as a "half a dozen guests
in a single room."[70] The excitement of life in Williamsburg was
evident everywhere:

> These were times of commotion and merriment to which
> Virginians thronged after months passed in the relative
> isolation of country life. They enjoyed fairs with puppet
> shows, contests of strength, beauty, dancing, and fiddling,
> footraces, and greased pig chases. This was also the height
> of the theater season, when . . . [a] Company of Comedians
> . . . presented rollicking farces . . . together with the more so-
> ber drama of Shakespeare and Joseph Addison. Horse races
> on the Quarter Path course just east of town and cockfights
> between the prize specimens from different counties of-
> fered diversion for all segments of society. Shopkeepers dis-
> played the latest European goods; slave auctions were held;
> lottery prizes were announced; and merchants gathered at

the open air Exchange near the Capitol to pay debts and con-
clude financial contracts.[71]

THE APPROACH OF REBELLION

By the mid-1760s, life in many of the American colonies along
the Atlantic coast began to take a serious turn. New British
policies such as taxing the colonists and other restrictive moves
by the Crown and Parliament were moving the colonies toward a state of rebellion. Virginia was not exempt from British
taxes. In 1765, when Parliament passed a tax on the colonies in
the form of the Stamp Act, colonists were up in arms. In Williamsburg, the House of Burgesses was wrapping up its spring
session when word of the Stamp Act reached the Virginia lawmakers. After a fiery speech by Patrick Henry, those burgesses
who had not already gone home passed a resolution of protest
against this new direct tax on its people. Despite such protests,
the act was scheduled to go into effect the following fall. When
the designated stamp distributor for Virginia, George Mercer,
arrived in Williamsburg in late October, he was met with a
mob demanding he resign his post. The resulting face-off became so intense that Governor Francis Farquier had to rescue
the besieged distributor and take him to safety at the Governor's Palace. By the next day, Mercer announced he would
resign as the Williamsburg residents had demanded. He was
immediately cheered by the crowd that had gathered.

As the 1760s became the 1770s, more clashes between the
House of Burgesses and British authorities took place when
unpopular acts, such as the Townshend duties, were thrust upon
the colonists. When the burgesses began a series of protests
against such taxes in 1769, the then-governor, Lord Botetourt, ended the session of the Virginia House. Undaunt-
ed, the ousted burgesses walked down the street and gathered at the Raleigh Tavern, and finished their session. Slowly,
but surely, the move toward a full-scale clash between the

colonies and Britain was approaching. Such burgesses as Thomas Jefferson, Patrick Henry, and others were corresponding with patriots throughout Virginia and in other colonies. When word reached Williamsburg in 1774 that Parliament had ordered the closing of Boston Harbor following the now-famous "Boston Tea Party," the Williamsburg burgesses voted for "a day of fasting, humiliation, and prayer."[72] This act and others led yet another governor, a Scotsman named John Murray, the Earl of Dunmore, to dissolve the House of Burgesses. Again, many of the burgesses merely moved down the street and took up their meetings at Raleigh Tavern. Even though such meetings were illegal, the burgesses soon gave their support to forming the Virginia Convention, from which delegates were chosen to "represent" Virginia in the intercolonial meetings of the Continental Congress, held in Philadelphia. Among those chosen were George Washington, Patrick Henry, Richard Henry Lee, Edmund and Peyton Randolph, and Benjamin Harrison.

TENSE MOMENTS IN WILLIAMSBURG

When the conflict between the colonies and the Crown slipped into full-scale war in the spring of 1775, Williamsburg became the site of an armed conflict. That spring, a British man-of-war, the H.M.S. *Fowey*, sailed up the York River, close to Williamsburg.

The members of the Virginia Convention left the town and took up meeting at a church in Richmond, about 50 miles inland. (It was there that the fiery Patrick Henry would deliver his now-famous speech that included the immortal words, "Give me liberty or give me death!")

Soon a struggle ensued over the weapons, gunpowder, and lead stored at the Williamsburg powder magazine. Governor Dunmore planned to move it all to the *Fowey*. On the night of April 20, 1775, British marines from the ship were sent to gather

In 1765, Patrick Henry delivered his famous "Caesar-Brutus" speech in opposition to the Stamp Act at the Capitol Building in Williamsburg. During the speech, he suggested that because England was impinging on America's freedom, King George III risked assassination, much like Julius Caesar. Ten years later, during a speech at the Virginia Convention's meeting in Richmond, Henry uttered the famous words, "Give me liberty or give me death!" in support of armed resistance against Great Britain.

up the cache of weapons and lead shot. They were detected, but managed to move the powder to the Governor's Palace. Although Patrick Henry and a group of 150 armed Virginians marched to the governor's house and demanded the return of the powder and shot, Governor Dunmore refused, offering instead to pay for it. The result was a standoff. Although the colonists did not get their powder back, Governor Dunmore's days in Williamsburg were numbered. Fearing for his life and that of his family, the Scot left the colonial capital by early June. He would be the last royal governor to reside at the Governor's Palace in Williamsburg.

8

A Colonial Settlement in Decline

With the opening of the Revolutionary War, Williamsburg's prominence would begin to decline. The last of the royally appointed governors had come and gone, replaced by true Virginians, such as Governor Patrick Henry, then Thomas Jefferson. Virginians played important roles in the events that comprised the Revolutionary War and the resulting separation and independence from Great Britain. Jefferson, after all, would write the document that became known as the Declaration of Independence. But other changes were coming to Williamsburg.

A NEW VIRGINIA CAPITAL

In 1780, during the Revolutionary War, the citizens of Williamsburg received some bad news. That year, the state's legislators decided to move the capital of Virginia again. Earlier colonial leaders had moved the capital from Jamestown to Williamsburg at the end of the 1600s. A new generation of leaders thought moving the capital to a new location, at Richmond, would make the capital safer for the remainder of the war. Once

During his term as governor of the colony of Virginia (1779 to 1781), Thomas Jefferson oversaw the transfer of the state capital from Williamsburg to Richmond. The relocation of the capital was responsible for the gradual decline in Williamsburg's prosperity, and by the early 1800s, the town was in disrepair.

Williamsburg ceased to serve as the capital of Virginia, its fortunes and future soon slipped into decline, just as those of Jamestown had nearly a century earlier.

One of those who had called for the removal of Virginia's capital from Williamsburg to Richmond was the colony's new governor, Thomas Jefferson. For several years, Jefferson had lobbied for the relocation of the commonwealth's capital. It was a change he thought was necessary. Such a relocation would encourage greater trade, because a move to Richmond would cause the colony's population to spread out farther, away from the coast. He even cited reasons that had been raised when the capital was moved from Jamestown, including a claim that Williamsburg's environment was unhealthy and that the capital was vulnerable to attack by Native Americans. Within two days of becoming governor, Jefferson managed to see that the colonial legislature passed a bill ordering the capital to be moved 50 miles away to Richmond.

DAYS OF DECLINE

Perhaps as a sign of Williamsburg's uncertain future, the Governor's Palace burned to the ground the following year. At that time, the governor's residence was being used as a hospital for patriot soldiers fighting in the Revolutionary War. Before the war ended two years later, additional buildings in Williamsburg were destroyed or damaged. Its decline began swiftly. A soldier from Pennsylvania, Ebenezer Denny, who was garrisoned in Williamsburg in 1783, took notice of the city's already obvious slide: "Williamsburg [is] a very handsome place, not so populous as Richmond, but situated on even, pretty ground; streets and lots spacious—does not appear to be a place of much business."[73] Two years later, the man who would be remembered as the compiler of one of America's first dictionaries, Noah Webster, passed through Williamsburg on a speaking tour. He could still see the former beauty of the town, but realized the community was changing for the worse, noting the same about the college, Bruton Parish Church, and the ruined capitol that they were "decaying, and so is the City, by reason of the removal of the seat of Government to Richmond."[74]

As the Revolutionary War and its aftermath brought the American colonial period to an end, so Williamsburg's colonial history faded with time. In 1816, a writer named George Tucker published a work titled *Letters from Virginia*. In it, he referred to Williamsburg in less than flattering terms:

> In short, this poor town has very little to recommend it to a stranger except the memory of its ancient importance, and this is but a sad sort of interest at best. There is neither business without doors, nor amusement within; but all is just as lifeless as the very Goddess of Dullness could wish.—Indeed, if it wasn't for the College, and the Court, and the Lunatics, I don't know what would become of it. As it is, it is but the shadow of itself, and even that seems passing away.[75] [Tucker's mention of "lunatics" refers to the Public Hospital, an asylum for the insane that had been built in Williamsburg in 1773.]

Eventually, no one living in the former Virginia capital had any memory of the glory days of Williamsburg with its tidy streets, well-run shops and taverns, and its sense of purpose as the center of all things political in Virginia. Throughout the nineteenth century, the fortunes of Williamsburg slipped further into the past. The town's well-built homes fell into ruin and general decay.

People sometimes altered the old colonial houses to update them or to make better use of them. Nearly all such changes were considered improvements on the former colonial structures. During the 1830s, Bruton Parish Church was redesigned and "modernized," including raising up new interior walls, moving the altar to the other end of the church, and creating a new entrance on the east side of the old building. Among those who attended the church at that time, there were those who called the redesign "a pitiable mistake."[76]

Other old symbols of Williamsburg's past did not even survive the nineteenth century intact. The Wren Building burned again, this time in 1859. It was built again, however, but the new version was much different in design from its predecessor. Bad luck continued to plague the college. The replacement of the Wren Building was interrupted by the Civil War and was not completed until 1869. But, by 1881, the college closed its doors, unable to receive adequate support or students. For seven years, the old college remained shut up, even as the college's president, Benjamin Ewell "faithfully tolled the college bell each September to commemorate the beginning of the fall term."[77] That same year, modern times arrived in the streets of Williamsburg as railroad tracks were laid down the center of Duke of Gloucester Street. While the tracks further marred the town's former colonial charm, the newly arrived trains brought tourists and sightseers.

A NEW FUTURE FOR WILLIAMSBURG

In time, as more and more of Williamsburg's colonial past slipped away, some residents decided to try and stop the decline. In 1889, more than a century after Williamsburg ceased to serve as Virginia's capital, a group of concerned citizens banded together and formed the Association for the Preservation of Virginia Antiquities (APVA). The group emerged from an effort that began five years earlier to "repair . . . tombs and walls in the churchyard at Bruton Parish Church."[78] The organization was formed by women, including the wife of Virginia's then-governor, Fitzhugh Lee, son of the Confederate general Robert E. Lee. The purpose of the group was to restore and

In the 1880s, a group of Williamsburg citizens formed the Association for the Preservation of Virginia Antiquities (APVA) to restore and preserve the town's historical buildings. The group's first preservation effort was to repair the tombs and walls in the courtyard of the Bruton Parish Church, which is pictured here.

preserve "buildings in which stirring deeds have been enacted, and where they have been destroyed to mark the spot on which they stood."[79] One of the important efforts this group mounted was the purchase of the old powder magazine, which the APVA fixed up and opened as a museum.

Other groups followed, including the Village Improvement Society, formed in 1907. (This organization was later called the Williamsburg Civic League.) Again, the members were local ladies who came together for the purpose of "improvement of civic conditions primarily with the view of making the place more attractive to the many visitors expected during the coming summer."[80] (That summer would mark the three-

---

THE MODERN WORLD REACHES WILLIAMSBURG

By the early twentieth century, Williamsburg was experiencing the effects of modernization. Despite all the worn-out reminders of its colonial past, changes were taking place to further separate the town from its heritage. Some old colonial sites were transformed by the needs of another generation of Williamsburg residents. On the site of the burned-out Governor's Palace, the town fathers had a new high school building constructed. One of the most important inns of colonial Williamsburg, the Raleigh Tavern, had become a general store. The once bustling center of the old town, Market Square, became crowded with a jumble of newer buildings, supermarkets, storefronts, and banks.

Duke of Gloucester Street had at one time served as the grand avenue of the colonial capital connecting the College of William and Mary on one end and the Capitol Building on the other. By 1901, the nearly 100-foot-wide thoroughfare was further altered by a line of telephone poles strung along the old street by the Chesapeake Telephone and Telegraph Company. In 1913, a new "Palace" was built and opened in Williamsburg, but it was not another residence for the governor. Instead, it was "The Palace," the town's first motion picture theater, built opposite the old Palace Green. By the 1920s, after the arrival of the automobile age in 1903, Williamsburg's old powder magazine was being used as a garage.

hundredth anniversary of the founding of nearby Jamestown.)
The group saw to it that several of Williamsburg's older buildings
were spruced up and painted. The ladies also clamored about
the telephone poles running down Duke of Gloucester Street,
but the poles did not come down until 1932, when the lines
were buried underground.

But these early efforts to salvage some of Williamsburg's
ancient past were merely small, cosmetic steps. The place
remained a mere shadow of itself in the early days of the
twentieth century, as George P. Coleman, a mayor from that
period, noted:

> Williamsburg on a summer day! The straggling street, an-
> kle deep in dust, grateful only to the chickens, ruffling their
> feathers in perfect safety from any traffic danger. The cows
> taking refuge from the heat of the sun, under the elms along
> the sidewalk. Our city fathers, assembled in friendly leisure,
> following the shade of the old Court House around the clock,
> sipping cool drinks, and discussing the glories of our past.
> Almost always our past! . . . The past alone held for them the
> brightness which tempted their thoughts to linger happily.[81]

THE DREAM OF DR. W.A.R. GOODWIN

By the 1920s, Williamsburg was still the home of nearly 100
buildings dating from the 1700s and 1800s. Some preservation
efforts, such as the Association for the Preservation of Virginia
Antiquities had been at work for more than a generation. Another group, the Catherine Memorial Society, had raised money
to renovate (yet again!) Bruton Parish Church. The work was
directed by Dr. William Archer Rutherford Goodwin, the rector
of the church. Goodwin had envisioned the restoration of the
Bruton Parish Church back to something resembling its days as
a colonial house of worship.

Dr. William Archer Rutherford Goodwin, pictured here in 1930, served as rector of Bruton Parish Church from 1903 to 1909 and again from 1926 to 1938. Goodwin was the driving force behind Williamsburg's restoration; in the 1920s, he began renovations on such historical landmarks as the George Wythe House and the old public jail.

Goodwin was a native Virginian, having grown up on a farm in Nelson County. He graduated from Roanoke College and Virginia Theological Seminary. His first ministry was as rector of an Episcopal church in Petersburg, south of Richmond. In 1903, he took the rectorship of Bruton Parish Church. But he stipulated that he would not take the post until the old church was restored back to its earlier colonial style. Once he made Williamsburg his home, Dr. Goodwin became one of the town's most respected citizens. As one of his friends would write: "He is . . . a man by whom the whole town seems to swear."[82] While he later served as a rector in Rochester, New York, Reverend Goodwin would eventually return to Williamsburg in 1923, after which he headed the Department of Biblical Literature and Religious Education at the College of William and Mary.

Restoring the town's colonial heritage became a burning passion for Reverend Goodwin. He was appalled that Williamsburg was becoming nothing more than just another "highway town lining a busy strip of concrete."[83] Williamsburg's past had been part of an important era in American history. The story was getting lost in the ever-encroaching world of the twentieth century. By restoring or rebuilding some of the important landmarks of colonial Williamsburg, Goodwin believed that people could make physical contact with their heritage. "It has been said that the best way to look at history is through windows," Goodwin wrote. "There are windows here, and there were others, which might be restored, through which unparalleled vistas open into the nation's past."[84]

After the successful renovations on Bruton Parish Church, other Goodwin-led restorations followed. An important colonial-era home, the George Wythe House (Wythe had been Thomas Jefferson's law teacher), built during the mid-1700s, was restored through funds raised by Goodwin and opened to the public in 1927. That same year, the old public gaol (jail) was renovated and opened to tourists. Goodwin spearheaded a project at the same time to purchase land around the old powder magazine to protect the area from modern development. The next year, the APVA offered the land where the Capitol Building had once stood (its foundations had been discovered underneath a cornfield in 1903) to the town fathers on the promise that the capitol would be rebuilt within the following five years.

Such an undertaking would require more money than the people of Williamsburg could possibly raise. It was only one more building on Goodwin's list of those he wanted to restore. He began making contacts with influential people outside the region. He wrote to the great automobile innovator Henry Ford, one of the wealthiest men in America. His approach was less than well thought out. In his letter, Goodwin accused the Ford family of having sped up the destruction of Williamsburg with the introduction of the automobile. "With the new concrete roads leading from Newport News to Richmond and with the road to nearby Jamestown passing through the city, garages and gas tanks are fast spoiling the whole appearance of the old streets and the old city, and most of the cars which stop at the garages and gas tanks are Ford cars."[85] Ford passed on Goodwin's request for money, sending the rector a letter in which he stated he would be "unable to interest himself in the matter mentioned."[86]

Reverend Goodwin continued his search. He took on a new fund-raising project to build a memorial hall on the College of William and Mary campus. While speaking to the New York City Chapter of the Phi Beta Kappa Society (the society was originally founded at Williamsburg's Raleigh Tavern in 1776), he came in contact with a wealthy man who would forever change the modern and colonial history of Williamsburg. In the audience that evening was the millionaire tycoon John D. Rockefeller, Jr. Afterward, he and Goodwin met, with the rector inviting him to Williamsburg. Rockefeller agreed

The George Wythe House, depicted in this 1892 painting by Dwight
Williams, was one of the first buildings in Williamsburg to be restored
by William Goodwin. Built in the mid-1700s, the residence was
the home of George Wythe, the country's first law professor and a
signatory of the Declaration of Independence.

and came to visit Goodwin, bringing along his wife and three
sons. The wealthy philanthropist toured Williamsburg, as well
as Jamestown and Yorktown. By 1926, the Phi Beta Kappa Memorial Hall was completed, and Rockefeller again returned
to Williamsburg for the dedication. Following a tour of the
George Wythe House, Rockefeller asked if he could walk
the streets of Williamsburg on his own. He did so, and that
evening, he announced at dinner that he was going to help

finance the restoration of the old colonial community, stating, "The restoration of Williamsburg . . . offered an opportunity to restore a complete area entirely free from alien or inharmonious surroundings . . . [that had] a unique and irresistible appeal."[87] He placed the project in the hands of an excited Reverend Goodwin.

9

New Life for Old Williamsburg

Reverend Goodwin did not wait long to take up the project of restoring the former colonial majesty of his beloved Williamsburg. In 1926, Rockefeller purchased his first Williamsburg home, the Ludwell-Paradise House, paying $8,000 after Goodwin telegraphed him that the house was for sale. (When Rockefeller answered the rector's telegram, he signed it "David's Father" to keep locals from knowing that a multimillionaire was buying houses in Williamsburg, which would cause prices to skyrocket. David was one of Rockefeller's sons.)

RESTORING THE PAST

Throughout most of the following decade, the project to renovate and restore colonial Williamsburg remained constantly in motion. An architectural firm, Perry, Shaw & Hepburn, was hired to spearhead the project, which Goodwin described to them as one that "would be the most spectacular and interesting, and from the teaching point of view, the most valuable restoration ever attempted in America."[88] Rockefeller remained

In 1926, John D. Rockefeller, Jr., agreed to finance the restoration and preservation of colonial Williamsburg. That year, Rockefeller purchased his first property, the Ludwell-Paradise House, for $8,000, and by 1934, the first phase of the renovation was complete.

directly involved in the project, which became one of his passions. By 1927, plans were underway to restore the Christopher Wren Building, the old capitol, the Governor's Palace, and the

In 1929, researchers discovered this copperplate engraving at Oxford University's Bodleian Library. The copperplate, which was used by architects as a template to re-create and restore Williamsburg's buildings, dates to 1740.

Golden Horseshoe Inn, one of colonial Williamsburg's taverns. The price tag was already nearly $1 million. By the spring of 1928, Reverend Goodwin had spent $2 million of Rockefeller's money buying nearly 40 of Williamsburg's colonial-era properties.

By February 1928, two companies were formed: Williamsburg Holding Corporation, to handle the business end of the restoration, and Colonial Williamsburg, Inc., a nonprofit organization to oversee the restorations and all educational activities. As the project gained momentum, it became clear to Reverend Goodwin that the Williamsburg public needed to be informed of what was happening and who was behind it all. Rumors were beginning to circulate. On June 12, 1928, a public meeting was held with the rector announcing that the

Rockefellers were providing monies to restore Williamsburg. At the meeting, Goodwin asked the townspeople if they would support the sale of public land in Williamsburg on behalf of the project. There were voices of opposition that day, including a townsman, S.D. Freeman, who warned that Williamsburg's residents might become "museumified," their town put on constant display, like "a butterfly pinned in a glass cabinet."[89] Of the 200 citizens present at the meeting, the vast majority favored the plan to revitalize and resurrect the history of their community, with only four opposition votes cast. For those citizens who did not want to sell their homes, Goodwin made them a special deal. They could live in their restored houses as "life tenants," paying only $1 rent each year.

A NEW LOOK FOR WILLIAMSBURG

By the end of the 1920s, the scope of the Williamsburg restoration project was ever-expanding. Those responsible for the physical restorations wrote out a list of "rules" for the restoration, called the "Decalogue." There would be no colonial-era buildings moved into Williamsburg from the outside. Everything later than the colonial period would be removed from all buildings, including later improvements or additions. Buildings should be restored or reconstructed on their original sites. (The difference between a building's "restoration" and its "reconstruction" should be explained. Colonial buildings that had survived into the twentieth century would be "restored" to their appearance during the 1700s. Buildings that had not survived, such as the Governor's Palace or the Capitol Building, would be rebuilt or "reconstructed" on their original foundations.) In just a few years, wrecking crews tore down more than 700 modern buildings sitting on colonial-era property.

By 1929, a department of research and records was organized to discover and study any historical papers or records

that would give restorers an idea of what the buildings of colonial Williamsburg actually looked like. This was not as easy
as it might seem. There were not always adequate records, including pictures, sketches, or engravings to show the actual
buildings. One of the most important documents used by restorers was called "The Frenchman's Map," which had prob-
ably been drawn by a French army officer who was in Virginia
in 1781 during the siege of Yorktown at the end of the Revolutionary War. This simple map presented an "aerial" view
of Williamsburg that showed the streets and the positions of
every one of the town's buildings. The map was found in the
library of the College of William and Mary in 1927. Those
working on the restoration project called the document the
"Bible of the Restoration."

Researchers and restorers studied anything they could get
their hands on, including old titles and deeds, wills, maps, earlier nineteenth-century photographs, drawings and sketches,
house and public building inventories, account books, personal
diaries and journals, and, especially, insurance policies. Such
policies might show the positions of buildings on a property, to
address the possibility of fire jumping from one building to another. The foundations of some outbuildings—structures that
might include summer kitchens, servant or slave quarters, laun-
dry buildings, privies (toilets), and such—were unearthed based
on locations given in insurance policies. Three such buildings
were eventually rebuilt on the George Wythe House property,
based on an 1801 insurance policy called a "Declaration of As-
surance." The John Greenlow House and its outbuildings were
built based on the same document.

One of the most dramatic rebuilding projects was the un-
earthing of the Governor's Palace foundations. Archaeologists
were called in and the excavation began in 1930:

> After the area was completely cleared, archaeologists dis-
> covered that foundation walls, steps, doorways, stone-paved

passages, and even the brick-walled boxes in the "Binn" cellar still survived. Many decorative as well as architectural features were derived from the evidence. The existence of walnut paneling in the main hall was determined from charred remains found in the debris. The hall floor of black and white marble slabs was based on excavated fragments. . . . Fragments of molded, rubbed, and gauged brick, lead-jointed stone steps, delft fireplace tiles, keys, hinges, shutter fasteners, and locks were also recovered.[90]

All this archaeological evidence was sifted and used to help provide clues for the materials to be used to rebuild the Governor's Palace.

While such materials were important, they did not tell restorers exactly what such buildings as the Governor's Palace looked like. In 1929, one of the most important discoveries connected to the project was made by researchers. An important engraving was found in the Bodleian Library at England's Oxford University. The copperplate dated to around 1740. A print from the plate revealed architectural drawings of some of the most important buildings at colonial Williamsburg, including front and back views of the Wren Building, along with the college president's house; the Capitol Building; and the Governor's Palace. A copy from the "Bodleian Plate" reached the architects at Williamsburg shortly after construction began. Work was already underway on the Wren Building and, based on the plate, the west side of the building's roof design was changed. Without this fortunate find, the work on restoring these buildings would have proven much more difficult.

A FRESH FUTURE FOR WILLIAMSBURG

The first renovated building open to the public was Raleigh Tavern, which was completed by the fall of 1932. (The original Raleigh burned down in 1859.) The Capitol Building renovations were finished by February 1934. Soon to follow was

Colonial Williamsburg has become a living history museum, where tourists can take a journey back to the 1700s. In addition to taking in the renovated and restored buildings, visitors can also view interpretive programs conducted by historians.

the Governor's Palace. By October 1934, the first phase of the project to restore colonial Williamsburg was largely completed. A special celebration was planned with President Franklin Roosevelt invited to come down from Washington, D.C., to speak. Everywhere, the work of nearly 10 years of restoration and renovation was apparent: Houses and public buildings had been reworked to appear as they had nearly 200 years earlier. There were homes, shops, and gardens on display, all intended to restore the spirit of an era thought to have vanished forever. (The colonial gardens planted throughout the newly reestablished Colonial Williamsburg neighborhoods covered more than 80 acres, filled with the types of plants known to have been planted during the eighteenth century.)

In his speech, President Roosevelt made note of the tireless work that had been completed:

> What a thrill it has been . . . to have the honor of formally opening the reconstructed Duke of Gloucester Street, which rightly can be called the most historic avenue in America; what a joy to . . . see the transformation which has taken place, to see the Capitol, the Governor's Palace, the Raleigh Tavern born again; to see 61 colonial buildings restored, 94 colonial buildings rebuilt; the magnificent gardens of colonial days reconstructed—in short to see how thorough the renaissance of these physical landmarks, the atmosphere of a whole glorious chapter in our history, has been captured.[91]

An elderly Reverend Goodwin was on hand during the ceremony, beaming with pride, dressed in his official vestments. He would give the president a personal tour of Bruton Parish Church.

The work continued throughout the 1930s with Reverend Goodwin always on hand, witnessing his vision of restoring the past come to life. John D. Rockefeller, Jr. remained equally involved, visiting Colonial Williamsburg twice each year. On each visit, he would walk the streets he had reestablished in time, giving directions concerning the gardens and which buildings could use new paint. As for Goodwin, he died in 1939. Rockefeller died in 1960, the work on Williamsburg still underway. By then, he had spent more than $100 million recreating his special chapter from the pages of Virginia's and America's history.

Throughout the twentieth century and on into the twenty-first, the work of restoring Williamsburg's former colonial majesty has continued. Research continues, and new work along Williamsburg's old streets not only keeps the memory but the reality of the past of this former colonial capital picture-perfect. Generations ago, Virginians walked these streets, greeted one another, gossiped about the latest news, drove their sheep, nailed public notices on the courthouse door, met in local taverns for conversation and a drink, hammered

COLONIAL WILLIAMSBURG: THE LEGACY CONTINUES

The work that brought about the revival of Colonial Williamsburg remains on display today. Millions of tourists descend each year on the re-created colonial community, paying a visit to the past. On their arrival, they find themselves transported into another time as they walk Duke of Gloucester Street, take tours of the gaol, the courthouse, the powder magazine, and the Governor's Palace, as well as dozens of other re-created sites. There is so much to see that visitors usually have to spend at least two days taking in the colonial capital from the Wren Building to the Capitol Building. Visitors leave their cars in the parking lot at Colonial Williamsburg. There are no automobiles allowed in the re-created city, only horse-drawn wagons, carts, and carriages.

Even though much of the work of restoration was completed in earlier decades, Colonial Williamsburg still employs a staff of 3,500, plus approximately 800 volunteers. These workers can be found operating the various shops and eating establishments. Some of them are modern-day craftsmen and -women, trained in a variety of skills and arts practiced during the colonial period from blacksmithing to soap-making to printing newspapers. In every house and home at Colonial Williamsburg, workers in period costume go about the business of keeping their homes, tending their gardens, washing their clothes, and feeding their animals. Over at Market Square, costumed "militiamen" carry out marching drills and practice loading and firing their muskets. Such workers are "interpreters" who tell visitors about what life was like in Virginia's capital during the 1700s. Some interpreters are dressed as the historical figures George Washington, Thomas Jefferson, and Patrick Henry. Colonial Williamsburg is a place where history comes alive.

Additional research and restoration continues today. Not only does a visit to Colonial Williamsburg include seeing the eighteenth-century buildings, horseshoes, tended gardens, drilled with muskets, passed laws, and created a world of their own making. Today, visitors may walk these same streets, witness these same often simple, sometimes significant acts, and relive this world that has been preserved for them and for future generations.

both public and private, that have been lovingly restored or reconstructed, it also features museums that have been established to enhance the experience. Such museums include the DeWitt Wallace Decorative Arts Gallery and the Abby Aldrich Rockefeller Folk Art Center. Both facilities are operated by the Colonial Williamsburg Foundation. Visitors to the DeWitt gallery enter through the reconstructed public hospital, the first public mental hospital built in America, in 1773. This facility was rebuilt and opened to the public in 1985, 100 years exactly after the original burned down. Some of the colonial restorations have been made at sites outside of Williamsburg proper. Tourists may visit a working plantation eight miles outside the colonial community called Carter's Grove.

Everything has been altered to remind visitors that they have stepped back into another time when they visit Colonial Williamsburg. A tourist stopping in at a tavern or inn will be offered drinks and food from colonial times. A meal might include crab cakes, Virginia ham, peanut soup, fried chicken, game pie, corn muffins, roasted potatoes, and Sally Lunn bread, along with special puddings. No detail is overlooked. Visitors do not spend modern money, but trade in their dollars for colonial money to spend in the shops and taverns.

Tourists can shop during their visit and take home something to remind them of the simpler times of the eighteenth century, including pewterware, dolls, newspapers, playing cards, baskets, tobacco and pipes, powdered wigs, bonnets, soap, jewelry, and candles. While all the items for sale are designed to reflect the past, the bygone era can even be seen in the boxes of animal crackers sold in the city. They come in the shapes of colonial-era animals, such as American cream draft and Canadian horses, American milking red Devon cows, Leicester long-wool sheep, and Hamburg roosters.

Chronology

1607 Jamestown, England's first permanent North American colony, is established; the settlement will become the first Virginia capital.

1633 First English settlers establish themselves at Middle Plantation; the site will be the future location of Williamsburg.

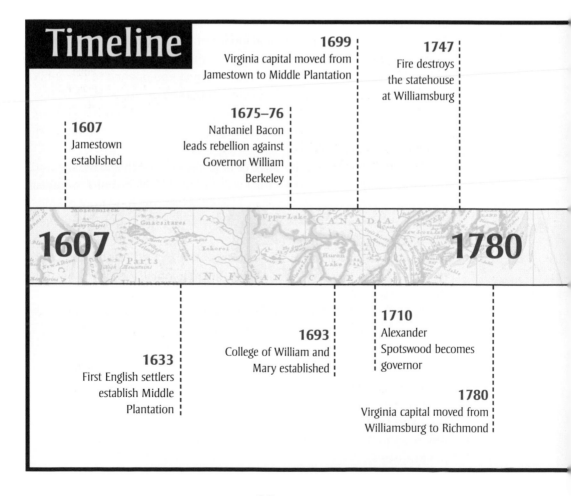

Timeline

1699
Virginia capital moved from Jamestown to Middle Plantation

1747
Fire destroys the statehouse at Williamsburg

1607
Jamestown established

1675–76
Nathaniel Bacon leads rebellion against Governor William Berkeley

1607

1780

1633
First English settlers establish Middle Plantation

1693
College of William and Mary established

1710
Alexander Spotswood becomes governor

1780
Virginia capital moved from Williamsburg to Richmond

1650 Planter John Page moves to Middle Plantation; he will become one of the settlement's leading citizens.

1675–76 Virginians, led by planter Nathaniel Bacon, engage in a rebellion against their governor, William Berkeley.

1677 William Berkeley is removed as Virginia's governor; with Jamestown destroyed by fire, Virginia burgesses meet at one of Middle Plantation's private homes; some Virginians begin campaigning to have the capital moved to Middle Plantation.

1830s
Bruton Parish Church is redesigned and "modernized"

1889
Association for the Preservation of Virginia Antiquities created to preserve Williamsburg

1926
John D. Rockefeller, Jr. agrees to financially back the restoration of colonial Williamsburg

1985
The Public Hospital is rebuilt and opened at Williamsburg

1830

1985

1859
Wren Building and Raleigh Tavern burn down

1907
The Village Improvement Society is founded to improve the appearance of Old Williamsburg

1934
Restoration and renovation of the Capitol Building is complete

1693 House of Burgesses authorizes the establishment of the College of William and Mary at Middle Plantation.

1695 Construction of the college's first permanent building is begun.

1698 The College of William and Mary opens its doors to its first students; that same year, yet another capitol building at Jamestown burns down.

1699 The House of Burgesses votes to move the capital from Jamestown to Middle Plantation, which will soon be renamed Williamsburg.

1705 Fire breaks out in the College of William and Mary's Wren Building, destroying it.

1710 A new governor arrives in Williamsburg, Alexander Spotswood; he will add important buildings and designs to the urban landscape of the capital, including a redesigned Bruton Parish Church, powder magazine, the Governor's Palace, and the Palace Green.

1715 Spotswood orders the construction of the powder magazine in Williamsburg; the redesigned Bruton Parish Church is completed.

1717 Raleigh Tavern opens in Williamsburg.

1722 Due to its growth, King George I declares Williamsburg to be a city.

1743 Wetherburn's Tavern opens for business in Williamsburg.

1747 Fire destroys the statehouse at Williamsburg.

1753 A new capitol building is completed at Williamsburg.

1773 The first public hospital for the mentally ill in America is opened in Williamsburg.

1780 Virginia legislators decide to move the capital from Williamsburg to Richmond.

1781 Williamsburg's Governor's Palace burns down.

1830s Bruton Parish Church is redesigned and "modernized."

1859 Wren Building burns down, as well as
Raleigh Tavern.

1869 A new Wren Building is finally completed.

1881 The College of William and Mary closes its doors;
the college will remain closed for the next seven
years; that same year, railroad tracks are laid
down the center of Duke of Gloucester Street.

1885 The Public Hospital, a facility for the mentally ill,
burns down.

1889 Concerned Virginia citizens form the Association
for the Preservation of Virginia Antiquities to try
to save Williamsburg's colonial heritage.

1903 Reverend W.A.R. Goodwin becomes rector of
Bruton Parish Church; he has a keen interest in
restoring Williamsburg's colonial heritage and
immediately takes up a project to revert Bruton
Parish Church to its colonial condition; that year,
the foundations of the old colonial capitol building are found in a local cornfield.

1907 The Village Improvement Society is founded to
improve the appearance of Old Williamsburg;
the organization will later be renamed the
Williamsburg Civic League; that year marks the
three-hundredth anniversary of the founding of
Jamestown.

1920s Williamsburg is still home to nearly 100 buildings
dating from the colonial era.

1923 After serving as rector of a church in Rochester,
New York, Reverend Goodwin returns to
Williamsburg, again as the rector of Bruton
Parish Church.

1926 Goodwin convinces millionaire John D.
Rockefeller, Jr. to financially back the restoration
of colonial Williamsburg.

1927 Through a Goodwin-led project, the
George Wythe House is restored and opened
to the public; plans are made to restore the
Christopher Wren Building, the Capitol Building,

the Governor's Palace, and the Golden Horseshoe Inn; fortunately, "The Frenchman's Map" is found in the library at the College of William and Mary; the map, drawn in the 1780s, shows the locations of many of Williamsburg's colonial buildings.

1928 Two companies are formed concerning the restoration of Williamsburg: the Williamsburg Holding Corporation and Colonial Williamsburg, Inc.; by June, the citizens of Williamsburg are informed that Rockefeller is backing the restoration of their town.

1929 A 1740 copper engraving plate is discovered in a library at Oxford University, England; the plate shows illustrations of some of Williamsburg's most important colonial-era buildings, including the Wren Building, the Capitol Building, and the Governor's Palace.

1932 Restoration on Raleigh Tavern is completed that fall.

1934 Restoration and renovation of the Capitol Building is completed; that year, President Franklin Roosevelt visits Colonial Williamsburg and declares Duke of Gloucester Street to be "the most historic avenue in America."

1939 Reverend W.A.R. Goodwin dies.

1960 John D. Rockefeller, Jr. dies; his legacy, the work at Colonial Williamsburg, continues to the present day.

1985 The Public Hospital is rebuilt and opened at Williamsburg.

Notes

Chapter 1

1. Allen Weinstein and R. Jackson Wilson, *Freedom and Crisis: An American History* (New York: Random House, 1974), 40.
2. Ibid.
3. Ibid.
4. Ibid., 41.
5. Ibid., 43.
6. Ibid., 45.
7. Harold B. Gill, Jr. and Ann Finlayson, *Colonial Virginia* (Nashville: Thomas Nelson, 1973), 55.

Chapter 2

8. Ibid., 56.
9. Ibid., 58–59.
10. Ibid., 59.
11. Ibid.
12. Weinstein, 51.
13. Ibid.
14. Ibid.
15. Gill, 61.
16. Ibid.
17. Ibid., 64.
18. Weinstein, 56.

Chapter 3

19. Michael Olmert, *Official Guide to Colonial Williamsburg* (Williamsburg: The Colonial Williamsburg Foundation, 1987), 11.
20. Gill, 66.
21. Olmert, 11.
22. Ibid.
23. George Humphrey Yetter, *Williamsburg Before and After: The Rebirth of Virginia's Colonial Capital* (Williamsburg: The Colonial Williamsburg Foundation, 1988), 14.
24. Robert P. Maccubbin, ed., *Williamsburg, Virginia: A City before the State, 1699–1999* (Published by the City of Williamsburg, 2000), 17.
25. Ibid.

Chapter 4

26. Ibid.
27. Ibid., 18.
28. Ibid., 19.
29. Ibid., 20.
30. Ibid.
31. Ibid., 21.
32. Ibid.

Chapter 5

33. Ibid., 21.
34. Ibid.
35. Gill, 68.
36. Ibid.
37. Ibid., 69.
38. Ibid.
39. Ibid.
40. Yetter, 14.
41. Gill, 77.
42. Ibid.
43. Yetter, 17.
44. Ibid.
45. Ibid.

46. Ibid.
47. Ibid.
48. Ibid.

Chapter 6
49. Yetter, 18.
50. Maccubbin, 17.
51. Gill, 81.
52. Ibid.
53. Hugh Howard, *Colonial Houses: The Historic Homes of Williamsburg* (New York: Henry N. Abrams, 2004), 9.
54. Yetter, 18–19.
55. Ibid., 19.
56. Gill, 83.
57. Yetter, 19.
58. Maccubbin, 33.
59. Ibid.
60. Gill, 83.
61. Ibid., 84.

Chapter 7
62. Olmert, 12.
63. Yetter, 108.
64. Ibid.
65. Ibid., 111.
66. Olmert, 42.
67. Ibid., 42–43.
68. Ibid., 43.
69. Dumas Malone, *Jefferson the Virginian* (Boston: Little, Brown & Company, 1948), 64.
70. Ibid., 63.
71. Yetter, 20–21.
72. Ibid., 24.

Chapter 8
73. Yetter, 32.
74. Ibid., 33.
75. Ibid., 34.
76. Ibid., 37.
77. Ibid., 42.
78. Ibid., 43.
79. Ibid., 44.
80. Ibid., 44–45.
81. Ibid., 45.
82. Ibid., 49.
83. Ibid., 50–51.
84. Ibid., 51.
85. Ibid., 51–52.
86. Ibid., 52.
87. Ibid., 54–55.

Chapter 9
88. Maccubbin, 181.
89. Richard Handler and Eric Gable, *The New History in an Old Museum: Creating the Past at Colonial Williamsburg* (Durham, N.C.: Duke University Press, 1997), 33.
90. Yetter, 65–66.
91. Ibid., 69, 71.

Bibliography

Andrews, Matthew Page. *Virginia: The Old Dominion.* Garden City, N.Y.: Doubleday, Doran & Company, 1937.

Beney, Peter. *The Majesty of Colonial Williamsburg.* Gretna, La.: Pelican Publishing Company, 1997.

Blackwell, Mary Alice, and Anne Patterson Causey. *Insiders' Guide to Williamsburg and Virginia's Historic Triangle.* Guilford, Conn.: The Globe Pequot Press, 2004.

Dufour, Ronald P. *Colonial America.* Minneapolis, Minn.: West Publishing Company, 1994.

Gill, Harold B., Jr., and Ann Finlayson. *Colonial Virginia.* Nashville, Tenn.: Thomas Nelson, 1973.

Handler, Richard, and Eric Gable. *The New History in an Old Museum: Creating the Past at Colonial Williamsburg.* Durham, N.C.: Duke University Press, 1997.

Howard, Hugh. *Colonial Houses: The Historic Homes of Williamsburg.* New York: Henry N. Abrams, 2004.

Maccubbin, Robert P., ed. *Williamsburg, Virginia: A City before the State, 1699–1999.* Published by the City of Williamsburg, 2000.

Malone, Dumas. *Jefferson the Virginian.* Boston: Little, Brown & Company, 1948.

Olmert, Michael. *Official Guide to Colonial Williamsburg.* Williamsburg: The Colonial Williamsburg Foundation, 1987.

Weinstein, Allen, and R. Jackson Wilson. *Freedom and Crisis: An American History.* New York: Random House, 1974.

Yetter, George Humphrey. *Williamsburg Before and After: The Rebirth of Virginia's Colonial Capital.* Williamsburg, Va.: The Colonial Williamsburg Foundation, 1988.

Further Reading

Alter, Judy. *"We the People": Williamsburg*. Minneapolis, Minn.: Compass Point Books, 2003.

Kalman, Bobbie. *A Colonial Town: Williamsburg*. New York: Crabtree Publishing Company, 1992.

Kent, Zachary. *Cornerstones of Freedom: The Story of Williamsburg*. Chicago: Children's Press, 1990.

McNeese, Tim. *The American Colonies*. St. Louis: Milliken Publishing Company, 2002.

Moore, Kay. *If You Lived at the Time of the American Revolution*. New York: Scholastic, 1997.

Samford, Patricia, and David L. Ribblett. *Archaeology for Young Explorers: Uncovering History at Colonial Williamsburg*. Williamsburg, Va.: The Colonial Williamsburg Foundation, 1995.

Web sites

Association for the Preservation of Virginia Antiquities
http://www.apva.org/

Guide for Historic Williamsburg
www.colonialwilliamsburg.com

Colonial Williamsburg
www.history.org/history

Bacon's Rebellion
http://www.nps.gov/archive/colo/Jthanout/BacRebel.html

Greater Williamsburg Chamber of Commerce
http://www.visitwilliamsburg.com/

Sir Christopher Wren Building
http://www.wm.edu/about/wren/index.php

Origins of the Williamsburg Restoration
http://xroads.virginia.edu/~UG99/hall/AMSTUD.html

Photo Credits

Index

About the Author

Series editor and author **TIM MCNEESE** is associate professor of history at York College in York, Nebraska, where he is in his fifteenth year of college instruction. Professor McNeese earned an Associate of Arts degree from York College, a Bachelor of Arts in history and political science from Harding University, and a Master of Arts in history from Missouri State University. A prolific author of books for elementary, middle, high school, and college readers, McNeese has published more than 80 books and educational materials over the past 20 years, on everything from Picasso to landmark Supreme Court decisions. His writing has earned him a citation in the library reference work *Contemporary Authors*. In 2006, McNeese appeared on the History Channel program *Risk Takers/History Makers: John Wesley Powell and the Grand Canyon*.